OSWEGO'S
CAMP HOLLIS

OSWEGO'S CAMP HOLLIS

Haven by the Lake

JIM FARFAGLIA

ILLUSTRATIONS BY TOM ROSHAU

THE
History
PRESS

Published by The History Press
Charleston, SC
www.historypress.com

First published 2021

Manufactured in the United States

ISBN 9781467145596

Library of Congress Control Number: 2021937198

OTHER BOOKS BY JIM FARFAGLIA

LOCAL HISTORY
In Pursuit of Clouds: The Journey of Oswego's Weatherman Bob Sykes
Nestlé in Fulton, New York: How Sweet It Was
Of the Earth: Stories from Oswego County's Muck Farms
Pioneers: The Story of Oswego County's Search and Rescue Team
Voices in the Storm: Stories from the Blizzard of '66

POETRY
The Best of Fulton
Country Boy
People, Places & Things: The Powerful Nouns of My Life
Reach Out in the Darkness: How Pop Music Saved My Mortal Soul

To Kathy Fenlon and Steve McDonough,
my Oswego City-County Youth Bureau directors,
who allowed me to fully express my love for Camp Hollis.

CONTENTS

ACKNOWLEDGEMENTS

I am grateful for the hundreds of Camp Hollis staff members I had the opportunity to work alongside. While I could not include everyone's name in this book, please know that your service to the camp and Oswego County children is part of this story. A record of those who've worked at the camp is featured on the Friends of Camp Hollis website. Click on its "Alumni" link to review the list.

One of the challenges in writing about a topic that spans nearly one hundred years is how to properly illustrate it. Since photographs of the Health Camp and Camp Hollis are from specific eras, I wasn't sure how to visually represent the universal aspects of a children's camp. When Tom Roshau, a Hollis staff member in the 1980s, shared cartoons he'd drawn about the camp, I knew that I'd found an answer to my problem. Along with a few photographs, Tom's art captures what it means to have attended or worked at a summer camp.

In addition, my thanks go to the following for their support during my research:

Ainsworth Memorial Library, Sandy Creek
Brenda Caster
Joyce Cook
Dave Dano
Donna DuBois-Taylor
Frank Fisher

Zach Grulich
Betty Hollis
Margaret Kastler
Minetto Historical Society, Kathy Mulcahey
New York State Department of Health
New York State Library
Oswego City-County Youth Bureau, Brian Chetney
Oswego County Clerk's Office, Christopher Jones
Oswego County Health Department, Jodi Martin
Oswego County Records Center, Justin White
Oswego County Tourism Department, Janet Clerkin
Sandy Creek History Center, Charlene Cole
The Eugene Sullivan family

THE ROAD TO CAMP HOLLIS

I first feel it, that rush of excitement, when I turn off State Route 104 onto County Route 89, trading highway traffic for a tree-lined country road. Most cars continue on 89 as it makes a right and heads toward Rudy's for a fish fry or Texas hot. But I continue straight ahead, where 89 becomes Lakeshore Road, better known by locals as Snake Swamp Road. Another quarter mile in the distance, through a break in the trees, I spot the lake, which, depending on the day, can be smooth as stone or angry as a witch's brew. Seeing the water assures me that I'm almost there.

My eyes are back on the road when I come to Snake Swamp's sharp bend to the left—how many counselors have nearly missed making that turn, foot heavy on the gas pedal, trying to get back to camp before curfew? Next comes a straight stretch of road lined with homes and manicured lawns, a far cry from how things looked many years ago. Christine Fisher had a window seat on the bus heading to camp in the 1950s, and she remembered that Snake Swamp Road "was so narrow the trees were coming in the windows! It became dark and the bus went silent with only the motor chugging."

Yes, back then, the ride felt like you were heading into wilderness, with any thoughts of city life snagged by those tree branches. But even today, after power lines and city water have tamed Snake Swamp, driving the next quarter mile or so through a marshy area still feels like I'm leaving one world for another. The road makes a small rise in elevation, lifting me out of the darkness, my destination now in sight.

At the top of the hill, a welcome sign guides me onto Health Camp Road, which is really just an extra-long driveway.* Gradually, the road narrows, its border of tall trees creating a canopy. Even on the brightest day, the world suddenly seems smaller, more precious, so I slow down. Sure, I'm watching for wildlife: deer, turkey, rabbits—once I came upon a good-sized snapping turtle taking its sweet time crossing the road—but I also slow down in anticipation. As I pass through a set of swinging metal gates and pull into a parking lot, I see what that patch of water a mile or so back was hinting at: Lake Ontario.

I turn the car off, and no matter my reason for visiting, I always take a moment to admire that Great Lake. The immenseness of Ontario still takes my breath away, but never more so than the day I viewed it from an airplane. It was the summer of 1975, and I was nineteen years old and already in love with Camp Hollis.

I owe that plane ride to Tom Wolbert, whom I met while working with his daughter, Karen Wolbert Allen (1975–80), at the camp. The ride took place on one of the few days off we had that summer; the job of a sleepaway camp counselor requires 'round-the-clock commitment. Often when we had a day away from camp, our staff would get together, many times at the Wolberts', where we would endlessly discuss our season in the sun. Tom must have overheard our talk and offered to give us a ride over the campgrounds in his two-seater plane.

One by one, we got our turn. I was plenty scared as I waited, having never flown before, and I can still hear Tom's chuckle as I grabbed my seat when we hit an air pocket. He wasn't laughing at me; he was showing me how to enjoy something a little out of my comfort zone. It worked, because I relaxed and began appreciating what I was observing. As we flew over the town of Oswego's wooded areas, I could see Lake Ontario beyond the trees. I knew Camp Hollis was down there somewhere, but I couldn't quite make out its buildings and ballfield. Tom probably wanted me to feel a little lost at that point, to surprise me with what I was about to see.

As he gently tilted the plane to the right, the clearing that was Camp Hollis appeared. From our altitude, it looked like a secluded village where the forest met the lake. I gasped; how incredible to see the camp, humble and peaceful. Until that plane ride, I'd only complained about the campground's

---

* Those whose history stretches back farther than mine will remember that the camp's original entrance was located off nearby West Lake Road. From there, a dirt path sent visitors along the lakeshore and then across a rickety bridge over a creek to the campgrounds. That bridge flooded so many times that the current entrance into camp was created.

Built in a wooded area in the town of Oswego, the camp's closest neighbor has always been Lake Ontario. *Courtesy of the Camp Hollis Archives.*

primitive conditions as I struggled to control groups of unruly children. Tom let the plane glide a minute or two, letting me appreciate the sight.

A few years later, at age twenty-two, I ended up running Camp Hollis—overseeing it, you might say—and that was a tremendous responsibility. I directed a staff of teenagers and twentysomethings who oversaw the care of young children, many away from home for the first time. This invited all kinds of drama, and emotions continuously ran high. I was a new leader trying to do my best, and I failed a lot. But slowly, year after year, season by season, I developed my style of directing.

Throughout my tenure with Camp Hollis, I thought back to that plane ride many times. When the job's challenges got to be their hardest and I couldn't think of any way on earth to solve my problems, I'd take a walk down to the shores of the lake and imagine myself in that plane, gliding above Camp Hollis. Seeing the big picture. Without fail, an answer to my concerns always came, as if it had been waiting for me, floating above that spot where the woods meet the lake.

I no longer run Camp Hollis, but whenever I visit, it feels the same, even when it looks different. Because no matter who I am when I reach that parking lot—a camper hopping off the school bus, a counselor ready to spend another summer dealing with children, a director worrying that the pool won't pass inspection or a volunteer ready to pull weeds in the camp gardens—it still takes my breath away. No matter where I reside, when I get to Camp Hollis, I'm home.

Thousands have considered it home, even though it may only have been for a few weeks or a few summers. Although counselor and Arts & Crafts director Ali Martin (2008–10) has never seen the camp from an airplane, her memories of working there sound like she has:

> *Weightless, I rise, hovering above the treetops.*
> *I look below me at ease, observing the sacred grounds beneath.*
> *Bonfires, giggles, discoveries and friendships;*
> *exploring, swimming, eating and playing.*
> *Generations pass and the blessed cycle continues on and on.*

With each cycle—there have been more than ninety so far—new counselors make memories as they move from childhood to adulthood in a single summer. Campers discover a previously unrealized talent, be it hitting an archery target or becoming a deep end swimmer. I heard it every camp season I worked there, and I'm sure it will be said this summer: "Camp Hollis changed my life." That's just what its founders had in mind.

A DOCTOR WITH A DREAM

O n the east end of Lake Ontario, in the town of Oswego, there is a cove, its crescent-shaped shoreline offering a quarter-mile walk on smooth rocks and sand. Bordering it, a bluff rises thirty or more feet—a towering fortress standing guard. Bank swallows have built nests in the bluff's crevasses for centuries, making them the first creatures to consider this inlet a refuge. In time, fishing boats found it a safe harbor from Ontario's storms, which are notorious for summoning deadly waves with a flash of lightning. By the late 1800s, townspeople from Oswego and city folk from Syracuse had discovered that by clearing a few trees near the bluff, they could enjoy summers in simple wooden cottages. News of such pleasure travels fast, and it found its way to northern Oswego County, to the village of Sandy Creek, where a country doctor was looking for just such a haven to protect children from a dreaded disease.

The good doctor was LeRoy F. Hollis, and he was well acquainted with that feared disease, tuberculosis. By the early 1900s, Dr. Hollis had witnessed how its crippling effects claimed the lives of many of his patients. He watched the infectious disease rapidly spread from community to community, its attack on the lungs earning it the nickname the "White Plague." Mention of it still sends a chill up the spines of those who remember when tuberculosis had no cure.

Although it did not discriminate in its victims, TB was especially cruel to the poor, who often lacked clean water and adequate housing. And while it's been a health threat as far back as recorded history stretches, it was during the onset of the Industrial Revolution, when overpopulated cities forced people into tight living quarters, that tuberculosis exploded into a major crisis.

By the end of World War I, with resources for healthy living conditions stretched thin, there were 1.2 million cases of TB in the United States, with 150,000 victims succumbing to its debilitating symptoms. When folk singer Jimmie Rogers recorded the song "T.B. Blues," many understood its lyrics all too well: "When it rained down sorrow," Jimmie lamented, "it rained all over me." In Oswego County, during the First World War and the years that followed, the number of newly infected TB sufferers hovered around 100 per year. By the late 1920s, the county's numbers were rising.

Medical researchers were working toward a cure for tuberculosis, but in the early twentieth century, effective medical treatment was still in its exploratory stage. As was true with other contagious diseases, for doctors like LeRoy Hollis, the only "remedy" they could offer their patients was prevention. At the first sign of the disease's symptoms—a persistent cough, difficulty breathing and walking or an unexplained loss of weight—doctors prescribed fresh air, nutritious meals and plenty of rest in hopes of building up weakened immune systems. To prevent further spread of tuberculosis, patients were placed in isolation: fathers were removed from their homes and mothers were separated from their children.

To provide this isolation, "resorts" were built, although that term is misleading. Imagine, rather, something of a maximum security prison, where the diseased were quarantined and their daily activities restricted. As cruel as those conditions sound, people saw it as their only hope for recovery. To express their faith in this health regimen, doctors gave these institutions a name derived from the Latin word *sano*, "to heal." Sanatoriums, medical professionals determined, were the best remedy for people threatened by the horrors of TB.

Although this was not a cure for tuberculosis, doctors nationwide noted improvements for those isolated in sanatoriums. As the number of cases rose, the need for those shelters increased, and to raise funds for their construction and maintenance, a charitable campaign was launched during the 1904 Christmas season. In keeping with the holiday spirit, a stamp, or Christmas Seal, became a thoughtful way to contribute to the fight against TB. Supporters bought them at a penny each to decorate Christmas card envelopes, and 4 million were purchased during the campaign's first year. New sanatoriums opened, including a popular one in Saranac Lake, New York, in the heart of the fresh air–filled Adirondack Mountains.

About 150 miles from Saranac Lake, at his office in Sandy Creek, Dr. Hollis studied the encouraging reports from the Adirondack sanatorium. Hollis believed that his patients, and all of Oswego County, could benefit from a sanatorium closer to home, and he began envisioning such a facility. The doctor had always been a forward-thinking man, evident even in his youth. When LeRoy graduated from Sandy Creek High in 1888, he became one of his hometown's first residents to further their education. Five years later, with a degree from Albany Medical College, Hollis was doctoring in Minetto, New York. A few years later, after receiving word that Sandy Creek was mourning the loss of its only doctor, he and his bride, Florence, returned to his hometown. LeRoy's medical expertise was warmly welcomed, as he recalled in a memorial booklet written to celebrate the Hollises' fiftieth wedding anniversary:

> *I was a young doctor and had to do and was expected to do the hard work and long drives out into the country. If the people saw you coming with your horse and buggy and wanted to see you, they had time to stop you.*

Indeed, Sandy Creekers' beloved doctor was quite recognizable, as George W. Corse pointed out in his town's newspaper column, "As I See It":

> *Ever since I was a little shaver I could look across the way and see "Doc" going about his calls…or to get the mail or serve the community in many ways that his capabilities made him fit to serve. He possessed a rare sense of humor and could crack a joke, even if the going was against him.*

Hollis made quite an impression during his travels in and about Sandy Creek. Lifelong resident Margaret Kastler remembered this about the doctor:

> *He drove a horse and buggy at first, then a new Buick when cars became popular. When he got so busy with his patients he hired a driver to take him from place to place. People would know if he was driving himself, though, because he always drove that Buick in first gear. You could hear him coming down the road.*

Margaret got a close enough look at the doctor to add this: "He wasn't a tall man, but stocky. He wore something known as spats, which were like a pair of stockings over shoes. They were a sign of high culture." Hollis's granddaughter by marriage, Betty Hollis, also noted the doctor's attention to detail: "He always wore a flower in his lapel."

Well dressed and somehow managing to drive his car from call to call, Hollis would carry on his Sandy Creek–based medical practice for nearly half a century, putting him face to face with the mounting epidemic of tuberculosis. In 1909, the State of New York took action, passing a law to provide funding for county tuberculosis hospitals. A year later, Dr. Thomas Carrington, of the National Association of the Study and Prevention of Tuberculosis, visited Oswego County, urging officials to form a committee to oversee a county-run sanatorium. Hollis pledged to lead the local effort and then recruited physicians and several elected lawmakers from Oswego County's Board of Supervisors.* Together they formed the Oswego County Committee on Tuberculosis and Public Health.

The committee's work was fruitful, and in October 1913, on a 160-acre farm on the western edge of the town of Orwell, seven residents were admitted to the Oswego County Sanatorium. By the end of its second year of operation, they had been joined by nearly one hundred TB sufferers.

For all the good being attempted at the sanatorium, some carry haunting memories of seeing their loved ones housed there in isolation. Margaret Kastler recalled what it meant to have a parent living there. As she rode with her family to Orwell, Kastler, a young child, was hoping to spend time with her mother, but "we had to talk to her through a screen door." Bob Green's memories are equally grim. When he was a teenager, Bob and his family traveled from Fulton to visit his older sister. "She took to shaking terribly and my father had taken her to the Sanatorium. After supper one night, she died of a heart attack. She was 21."

By 1917, Dr. Hollis had been appointed superintendent of the Oswego County Sanatorium, although it meant giving up his Sandy Creek medical practice.† Although Hollis was pleased with the sanatorium's expanding level of care, he had a special concern for one group of patients: children. While the disease affected all ages, it was youngsters' still-developing lungs that made them especially vulnerable. The Orwell Sanatorium provided children the same treatment—fresh air, clean water and plenty of nutritious food— as it did for adults, but the facility lacked the playfulness a growing child

---

* In 1947, the Board of Supervisors became known as the Oswego County Legislature.

† LeRoy's townspeople needn't have been concerned that they were losing their doctor. When he began his new position, Hollis's son, Harwood, a recent graduate from Syracuse Medical College, became the second Dr. Hollis to keep Sandy Creekers healthy. A third Hollis, LeRoy's grandson Warren, would also serve as Sandy Creek's loyal physician.

Dr. LeRoy Hollis *(far left)* led the efforts to establish the Oswego County Sanatorium, a facility for those fighting the deadly effects of tuberculosis. *Courtesy of the Hollis family.*

needs. Given Oswego County's pleasant summer weather, Hollis and his committee considered establishing a site where, as a 1924 *Sandy Creek News* article described it, "delicate children can spend a few weeks under trained supervision that their health may be brought up to normal."

Hollis knew the benefits of recreation for children, having volunteered for the Boy Scouts and a Fresh Air–style camp for Syracuse youngsters at Lake Ontario's Sandy Pond beaches. After learning the results of other recreation programs for children at risk of contracting tuberculosis, he was convinced that such a program should be the next step in Oswego County's battle against the disease. In a 1930 essay, Hollis reflected on what convinced him that his county's children needed their own facility, which were being referred to as "health camps":

> *In 1909, there was established in Farmingdale, New Jersey, an institution to care for pre-tuberculosis children, those undernourished, having been exposed to the infection of tuberculosis and who, unless their resistance could be built up, were good prospects of developing tuberculosis. The children have been taught certain fundamental rules of hygiene, how to play, how to rest, how to sleep and how to conserve their energy.*
>
> *Since that time, nearly every county in this state, as well as other states, have established camps where the undernourished children of pre-tuberculosis type could be sent for six to eight weeks under proper supervision.*

One of the health camps Hollis referred to was Camp Oakwood, which opened in 1923 at Sodus Point, thirty miles west of Oswego County. The camp was for children between the ages of five and eighteen who were "suffering from malnutrition or living in families where there is active tuberculosis." Hollis noted an additional requirement used to determine a camper's eligibility for attendance: "This is not a convalescent home for children who are sick or recovering from some illness, but rather a playground for the child free from disease whose general condition needs building up."

As he rallied support for an Oswego County health camp, Dr. Hollis made sure to point out that the Oakwood camp "is intended to reach particularly children whose parents cannot afford to send them away for a vacation." With that, he decided that his camp would be free of charge. Although this would mean increasing its fundraising efforts, the Oswego County Committee on Tuberculosis and Public Health agreed with the doctor, and the search began for an appropriate camp site.

In 1925, James E. Lanigan, chairmen of the Health Committee, announced the good news. The site for Oswego County's new health camp had been secured. It was a farmhouse in Volney Center, situated on the rural Mexico-Fulton Road. Owner Mrs. W.P. Kitty (or Kittie) Gass gave the committee a tour of her brick home, which was positioned on a knoll and sat well back from the road. A grove of trees could offer afternoon shade, she mentioned, while windows on the house's second floor, where the children would sleep, provided plenty of sunlight.

Committee members turned their attention to staffing the camp. Eleanor McCully, of Fulton, was named the health camp's director, and Miss Lillian Moore, RN, having provided care for TB-infected children at the Oswego County Sanatorium, became the camp's medical supervisor. The *Pulaski Democrat* offered a succinct description of the ideal camper: "Underweight and convalescing children from six to fourteen, who are in need of a vacation under supervision and care….No contagious or infectious cases are accepted."

But before any needful child could enjoy a summer vacation, the committee had to turn the farmhouse into a recreational camp. With no local budget for such a venture, the county put out a call for necessary supplies ranging from indoor furniture—the camp especially needed beds—to sports equipment. Post-season reports indicate that in that first summer, the camp operated primarily with food donations and loaned necessities. What couldn't be borrowed to run the camp's six-week schedule was covered by Christmas Seal sales, which contributed just over $1,000 (present value: $13,700).

When the first campers arrived, on July 6, 1925, their initiation to summer camp looked a lot like it does today. Before the fun could begin, a health checkup was conducted, including an examination to rule out everything from dangerous contagious diseases to pesky head

lice. But unlike children today, the boys and girls attending the Oswego County Health Camp had to complete one additional step: a step onto a scale. Since a robust physical condition was an important component in fighting TB, each camper's weight was recorded at the beginning and end of their stay. Dr. Hollis's camp would be considered a success if, as Nurse Moore proudly reported at the conclusion of that first summer, "every child at the camp has gained in weight."

Twenty-nine children who enjoyed sunshine and shade, breathed in lungfuls of fresh air and ate to their heart's content were encouraging signs for the health camp's ambitious goals. Dr. Hollis and Oswego County's TB and Public Health Committee found the news encouraging enough to give their experimental camp a second season. Again held at the Volney farmhouse, 1926's four-week camp was supported by a number of charitable events, including one that produced this newspaper headline: "One Hundred at Silver Tea at Health Camp."

Those attending the tea witnessed the camp in operation. "They found children contented and happy and getting back to normalcy," the reporter noted. Then, shifting from specific details to persuasive editorializing, the article suggested, "If you haven't been yet, go and see what the County Association and those in charge of the camp are doing for the rising generation. It will be a revelation to you along the lines of home missionary work and a real demonstration of the Golden Rule." When ads began to appear for that season's Christmas Seal sales, they included this inspiring scenario:

> *Bright eyes and tanned happy faces, laughter and fun are all gifts the Christmas Seal gave this year to little children in Health Camps in 27*

counties of New York State. Sharing in the happiness, bodybuilding and character-forming activities of these camps this past summer were 1,180 boys and girls.

Among those lucky campers were thirty Oswego County children.

Buoyed by reports of the Oswego County Health Camp's youngsters growing stronger, the program returned to the Gass farmhouse for the 1927 season. Success was gauged by one reporter who followed the camp to an outing at Ontario Park, on the lake in Oswego: "Campers played, gobbled up ice cream and returned to camp, tired, but smiling." However, during the summer, staff grappled with the farmhouse's lack of an adequate water supply. Potable water was hauled to the site, and after a trying six-week camp session, the county's Health Committee acknowledged that the Volney site could not meet their stringent health standards.

Before discussing the uncertain future of their Health Camp, committee treasurer L.W. Emerick, of Fulton, reported total 1927 program expenses of $1,120.75. Dr. Hollis then offered evidence of money well spent with these facts: forty-nine children were served—twenty from Oswego, sixteen from Fulton and thirteen from elsewhere in the county. Those youngsters left the camp, Hollis pointed out, with something they hadn't come with: an average gain of six pounds. The news was too good to ignore. The committee vowed to find a new site for their health camp.

By December, their search ended with a visit to a three-acre plot of undeveloped land situated at Lewis's Bluff on Lake Ontario in the town of Oswego. Owner Joseph Glerum was asked by the committee to give them a ninety-day option to meet his asking price of $1,000. Additional funds to prepare his property for the camp would be covered by ramping up Christmas Seal sale appeals. A newspaper article listed the reasons why committee members were so enthusiastic about their find:

> *The property is ideally located for a health camp....The site is easily accessible, and electric and telephone lines can be carried to the place.... The lake shore is shallow and a sandy beach makes it favorable for bathing, while the high bluff on one side affords an excellent place for the camp buildings.*

Although the report failed to mention another desirable quality found at Lewis's Bluff, those responsible for the Health Camp's activities would have noticed this: standing on the edge of the bluff, facing the lake, one could

visualize the evening campfires to be held there. Songs and stories (both jovial and scary) could be shared with children gathered around a fire circle. As dusk set in, with campers huddled close to their counselors, the camp director could point out something in the distance. Gazing out over the lake, on the horizon, those first boys and girls to enjoy the Lewis's Bluff camp would witness what many have called the most beautiful sight in the world: a Lake Ontario sunset.

THE DREAM FINDS A HOME

In order for children to enjoy campfires, sunsets and more at Lewis's Bluff, the Oswego County TB Committee spent the winter of 1927 and spring of '28 figuring out how to turn a dense patch of woods into a campground. The committee, now known as the Oswego County Health Association Inc., announced the revised specifics of its mission: "To deal with public health [and] cooperate with the New York State Health Department and the State Charities Aid Association to eradicate tuberculosis." But the first item on the new Health Association's list of priorities didn't have much to do with promoting health. Instead, the group found itself in the construction business.

By May 1928, the Association had settled on a contractor for the Health Camp's summer home. Frederick A. Montayne, of Lacona, submitted the winning bid, guaranteeing to complete the structure for $5,390 (more than $80,000 today). When announcing the cost, the Association noted that all building expenses were to be covered by Christmas Seal sales, adding several thousand dollars to its already substantial goal. Montayne's blueprints showed a building comprising three sections. A center room, measuring fifty by twenty feet, would accommodate a large dining area, a restaurant-style kitchen, an administration office and an isolation room, where a single bed could accommodate a child showing symptoms of a contagious disease until a doctor could be summoned. On either side of that center space, set off at angles, were the boys' and girls' dormitories, each measuring fifty by twenty feet. Adjacent to the new building, plans included a holding tank for well water and a septic tank for waste.

Windows in the Health Camp's dormitories were intentionally large in order to provide plenty of fresh air, an important component in strengthening a child's immune system. *Courtesy of the Sullivan family.*

Those overseeing the new construction most certainly had no idea that their building would remain the hub of camp life at Lewis's Bluff for fifty-five years. Many who attended or worked at the camp prior to 1984 can still walk through that building in their mind. The long dormitories held rows of beds, and each had a thin wall at one end to give counselors a small private sleeping area. Each dorm's bathroom housed three toilets, two sinks and one bathtub (later converted to a shower), giving campers a great opportunity to practice patience. One feature of the dorms was custom built for a health camp: nearly every inch of wall space was fitted with large windows, providing the vital fresh air needed in the fight against TB.

Sandwiched between the dormitories, meals were prepared and served, a small closet held supplies and even smaller spaces housed the director and nurse stations. Everybody hoped for sunny days since there wasn't a lot of

Architects of the Health Camp's main building included plans for an indoor fireplace, which provided warmth and comfort during inclement weather. *Courtesy of the Camp Hollis Archives.*

leg room indoors. But if rain fell or the lake delivered a late summer chill, the new building would be prepared. Included in Montayne's plan was an indoor fireplace. Built using lake stone and topped with an oak mantelpiece, it offered a cozy nook where children could enjoy a warm breakfast on cold mornings or counselors could lead campfire songs to drown out a thunderstorm.

Aside from Montayne's being the low bid, the Health Association liked another guarantee he wrote into his proposal: he promised that the new building would be ready for occupancy by July 1, 1928. The Association got a boost from local media, which announced the need for increased Christmas Seal sales. "Right here is where churches, social and fraternal associations can show their interest in the project and come forward with the helping hand," one editorial proclaimed, "so that the full capacity of the health camp may be available now."

Donors responded financially, but also in other meaningful ways. To supplement the twenty-five beds already owned by the Health Association, Fulton's school board loaned another thirty. Mrs. Al Edwards of Oswego presented a bedroom set for the camp director's room, and a group of Hannibal women provided a dozen bedsheets. The Wednesday Club of Sandy Creek added thirty-six more bed linens by holding a benefit picnic. An Association subcommittee—comprising members Thomas McKay, Mrs. James Feeney and E.M. Waterbury—addressed the camp's equipment needs by securing cooking and refrigeration units.

None of that generosity would have mattered without electricity, and with just a month left before the first campers would arrive, the site was still without power. Funds were scraped together, and by the end of June, the

People's Gas and Electric Company had sent a crew to string a line from a Lewis's Bluff neighbor, bringing the Health Camp to life.

Throughout the construction phase, the recruitment of children was underway. An Oswego County health nurse announced the camp's eligibility guidelines. They were looking for boys and girls from a TB-inflicted family or neighborhood who tipped the scales at least 10 percent under their ideal weight.

The final task—many would suggest it was the most important work the Health Association was expected to accomplish—was the hiring of qualified staff. Health Camp subcommittee member Mrs. James C. Feeney, of Oswego, would be the program's director; meals would be prepared by Mrs. Lena Gifford and her assistant, Mrs. Ida Parsons; and Drs. H.L. Albertson, E.S. Arthur and LeRoy Hollis were to examine the children entering camp and ensure their well-being throughout their stay. Serving in the role of "play director," a position that would soon be better known as counselor, were two students enrolled at the Oswego Normal School (precursor to the State University College at Oswego), Elizabeth Pettigrew and Rosemarion Fitzgibbons. Many years later, Rosemarion recalled that summer in 1928, which she admitted was the first time she ever stepped foot on a campground:

> *We were responsible for the entertainment and well-being of 45 to 50 children who ranged in age from 4 to 14. I can't remember that we had any playground equipment at all. We had to do everything for those children. Imagine the two of us pouring all that milk at each meal. The entire staff was female, so at night the Director's husband, Mr. Feeney, came to camp to sleep so that there would be a man on site.*

Rosemarion earned $100 for her summer's work, but she remembered receiving something greater. As a college student anticipating a career in teaching, she noted that "I learned my first lessons in discipline at the Health Camp."

A newspaper article covered that first summer at Lewis's Bluff by describing a typical day: flag raising, breakfast, cleanup, morning swim, free play, dinner ("Teeth are brushed before and after each meal"), nap time, another swim, free play and supper at six o'clock. Evenings were devoted to a campfire songfest. Bedtime was eight. Rosemarion recalled a few special events, like the day the camp "got a city bus and took the children to the movies and got them ice cream."

Not every reportable event that first summer was pleasurable for youngsters, but they were critical to the camp's success. Fifteen children who had never been treated were given toxin-antitoxin for the prevention of diphtheria and all campers received nightly exams to prevent the spread of contagious diseases—poignant reminders of the reason for all that fun.

The Health Association had a little fun with its July report on the children's progress: "All campers have gained one and three-quarters pounds since July 10…a record which the Children's Health Camp at Lewis's Bluff prizes as much as Babe Ruth does his home run average." Tuesdays became weigh-in days, and they were almost ceremonial. Every camper was to "mount a little white platform and anxiously watch the weight on a bar being moved up notch by notch." Cheers were extra loud when, as reported, "some children have gained as much as three pounds."

Other important numbers helped define the first season at Lewis's Bluff. Seventy-one children were cared for; fifty-three stayed the entire six weeks. A breakdown of the campers' hometowns provided evidence of the Health Committee's commitment to serve the entire county: eighteen children from Oswego; seventeen from Fulton; seven from Schroeppel and Phoenix; six from Mexico; five from Richland; three each from Sandy Creek, Minetto and Hannibal; two each from Orwell, Albion, Williamstown and Oswego Town; and one from New Haven. But it was back to the scales for the most prized numbers. Dr. Hollis himself proudly noted that "*all* children greatly improved by gaining an average of 6 healthy pounds to their undernourished bodies; one added a remarkable 11 pounds."

That extra weight was seen as an added defense when the campers returned home, especially when Hollis announced that tuberculosis "no longer need be considered an incurable ailment." The doctor told stories of children who'd had full recoveries, emphasizing what he believed was key to eventually defeating tuberculosis: early diagnosis and proper preventative measures. Tuberculosis "often occurs in families which have large numbers of children," Hollis explained, "where family income is insufficient, and where proper food is lacking." Now, after its fourth successful season of serving youngsters in Oswego County, the doctor could refer to his Health Camp "as a most valuable adjunct to the Sanatorium in preventing many cases of tuberculosis."

Encouraged by this hopeful news, December 1928's Christmas Seal sales goal for Oswego County was set at seventy-five thousand stamps, although the $750 it would raise was a far cry from the funds still needed to pay off the new building, purchase much-needed supplies and add a few pieces of playground equipment. Additionally, there would be the $2,000 to prepare for next season's food and staffing and $1,200 to cover essential medical services. It seemed an insurmountable sum of money to raise, but the Health Association had an idea.

Its plan was to reach out to the entire county of Oswego, town by town. All municipalities would be challenged to appoint their own committee to advocate for the Health Camp, with each group spearheaded by a community leader. In Oswego, former county judge Francis D. Culkin took the helm. In Fulton, Mrs. Charles Swain was committee chair. Mrs. Joseph T. Bond assumed that role in Phoenix, and Mrs. Ella More did so in Pulaski. Support didn't stop at the county borders; Kiwanis International pledged its 1929 support to five hundred health camps nationwide, including Oswego County's.

To boost the plan's chance for success, Dr. Hollis contributed to its fundraising efforts, including a presentation to Oswego County's governing body, the Board of Supervisors. At the conclusion of Hollis's inspiring report, the supervisors approved an appropriation of $1,650 for his Health Camp, marking the first time support of the Lewis's Bluff camp appeared as a county budget line item. From that point on, providing a healthy camp experience for children remained an important matter for Oswego County lawmakers.

Creative fundraising efforts continued. In 1930, the city of Oswego's State Armory hosted a Boy Scouts of Oswego County exhibition. To view the Scouts' outdoor life skills and badge-earning projects, adults were charged twenty-five cents and children a dime. As visitors offered their coins, they passed a poster outlining the Scouts' charitable intent: "Money raised will benefit the Health Camp at Lewis's Bluff's playground equipment fund."

Unfortunately, an incident at the camp over the winter added to the committee's fundraising challenges. Upon opening in the spring, camp staff discovered silverware missing. Who would attack a camp dedicated to serving the poor, especially when Oswego County nurses made this report to the Health Association: the number of children they would recommend for the 1930 summer session far exceeded the camp's capacity. In Fulton alone, the nurses advised, forty-three children were in need of services. The Oswego city tuberculosis nurse recommended twenty, and her county-wide counterpart recommended seventeen. All the children met the low weight and exposure to TB criteria, forcing the camper selection committee to undertake the unpleasant task of determining who had the greatest need.

Buildings and grounds issues at Lewis's Bluff put additional pressure on the fledgling camp. By the close of its third season, its water supply had proved to be consistently unreliable. A new well would have to be dug—or at least, that's what camp administrators thought. Longtime Camp Hollis neighbor Charles Groat remembered that something beyond digging needed to be done. "They had to go down 84 feet to hit potable water," Groat explained. "To find it they had to drill through solid rock." The *Sandy Creek News* explained the importance of the camp's new water system: "While on a smaller scale, [it] will be identical in theory and operation with those now installed in most cities to protect their sources of water supply. It will guard against the spread of any form of waterborne disease in the camp."

While county health inspectors made sure that the camp's drinking water was potable, they couldn't do much about the strong smell that came with every glassful. Scientists knew that the odor was caused by high levels of hydrogen sulfide gas, or sulfur, in water levels, but campers and staff had a more accurate description: it smelled like rotten eggs. Kitchen staff did their best to mask the unpleasant odor by offering gallons of "bug juice": the foul water laced with Kool-Aid.

Amid all the camp's health challenges and financial concerns, Duane E. Fairchild's donation must have seemed like a breath of fresh air. The Oswego resident contacted the camp to offer his piano, and for the staff who led daily singalongs, it was a joyful contribution. Eighty-six children raised their voices with that piano in the Health Camp's third season—thirty-four boys and fifty-two girls. All were under the age of twelve, and they were guided by an attentive staff through music, outdoor play, bug juice breaks and, of course, unlimited food. In what was now an annual end-of-summer announcement, on average, campers left for home carrying an extra six pounds.

A July 1931 announcement of the camp's fourth season introduced its new director, Martha Foot, of Oswego. A recently certified school nurse/teacher, Miss Foot came to the camp with two years' experience at a Palmyra, New York high school. Like others in the education field, Martha needed a summer job, and after a friend suggested she consider opportunities in recreation, she applied to the Health Camp. In 1997, sixty-six years after her first summer on Lewis's Bluff, Martha shared vivid memories of why she considered devoting five summers to children one of the best decisions she ever made:

> *Mr. John Henry, attorney, was the Chairman of the Oswego County Health Association and he convinced me that, instead of being a counselor, I should accept the position as Nurse Director of the Camp. This meant supervision of the staff, executing the health regimen for the children and responsibility of the kitchen and recreational programming.*

A regular schedule was maintained: meal time, play time, program time, and water sports. There were volleyball, baseball and table tennis games. A highlight of one summer was when the midget from Barnum and Bailey Circus came to entertain. We sang too—how we loved to sing! Robert Oliver, student at Syracuse University, led us.

Much time was taken for water safety, supervised by Matt Barclay, later a physical education teacher in Oswego. My time at the camp was during the height of Prohibition and we suspected boats coming into one cove at the foot of the bluff were landing illegal whiskey. One morning, our boat was missing and the Palladium-Times gave us wonderful publicity. Its headline read: "Who would steal a rowboat from a Health Camp would steal candy out of a child's mouth." The rowboat was returned the following night.

Robert Allison, also a board member and a wholesale grocer, agreed to help me with ordering on a large scale. Menu planning was no problem. Mrs. Lela Burton, of Oswego, was a splendid cook and manager who worked for us for [my entire time] there. At that time, Roy Tovey, a student also from the college, was her assistant. Both the staff and campers thrived on Mrs. Burton's nutritious meals.

The children always seemed to be hungry and gained pounds and pounds. We had a large ice refrigerator in the kitchen—no freezers in those days. Pasteurized milk was delivered by Las Vij's Dairy in Oswego and kept in a cooler. Our neighbors were generous; at times they gave us fruit and vegetables from their gardens. The biggest challenge was deciding how to use a bushel of cucumbers. They were good creamed.

Ms. Foot noted that campers were recruited by Miss Lucy Vincent, a TB nurse from the Sanatorium, as well as through county schools. As a school nurse/teacher, Martha conducted the health checks:

> *Children with head lice were not accepted and we weren't supposed to take bed wetters, but, as the children's ages were from six to twelve, we got a few. There was bath time, too. There were no shower heads; we used spigots the children stood under and were scrubbed or helped. We had [cleanliness] competitions, such as the best made bed, etc. After flyswatters were passed out, an award was given for the most flies killed. Sounds horrible now, doesn't it, but window screening was poor.*
>
> *The staff consisted mostly of students from the college at Oswego: Phil Fleischman, Rosemarion Fitzgibbons, and Elizabeth Pettigrew; plus Mary Summerville of Fulton and Virginia Hardy of Sandy Creek. I must not neglect to name Al Nancetti, of Utica, who was with us for three years and stayed during the entire season. They enjoyed the children, as I did, and some of those children even loved us!*

At the end of the 1931 season, the children's families were guests at a celebratory picnic and program, including a play with an intriguing title: *The Camp Director's Nightmare*. Although the play's storyline remains a mystery, it's safe to venture that it holds the honor of being the first skit ever performed at Lewis's Bluff. This was followed by renditions of the campers' favorite songs, and then awards were announced, with each lucky winner receiving a wristwatch. Most of the awards were health-based, including the cleanest plate, brownest tan and neatest girl and boy. Of course, the grand prize went to the camper who'd gained the most pounds. That summer, Doris Dumas, of Minetto, tipped the scales in her favor, with a hearty ten and a half additional pounds.

Among the most encouraging news from 1931 was that sixty-one campers enjoyed the full summer session, with ninety-four children served in total. Officials noted that the camp was at capacity at all times and that a new child could only enter when one went home. The only problem, they admitted, was homesickness. Staff noticed that when parents showed up for visiting day on Sundays, it proved too much for some children and a few left with their families. Later in the summer, those children asked to return, but their space had been filled. By the next summer, a new rule was in place: Sunday visits would be limited to two hours.

Despite the success of the little camp on the lake, Oswego County, as well as the rest of the United States, had bigger concerns. Our country was in the grips of the Great Depression. A December 1931 issue of the *Fulton Patriot* reported that local Christmas Seal sales had fallen nearly $500 (from $3,787.65 in 1930 to $3,228.60 in '31), causing Mrs. John Parsons, the Health Association's sales chairperson, to make this ominous prediction: "Unless the proceeds from the sale are considerably increased so they will finally approximate last year's total figure, the work of carrying on the children's health camp at Lewis's Bluff, dependent solely upon the Seal sale for its support, will be seriously interfered with and the program may have to be curtailed."

Mrs. Parsons's warning was heard. The Health Camp did open in 1932, but those operating the camp still had to contend with significant financial challenges, including the elimination of an Oswego County nurse who had handled much of the camper recruitment. That task became the responsibility of city and town health officers, who, along with caring for their constituents' medical needs, were now required to transport children to and from the camp.

Despite Depression-era shortfalls, in 1933, the Oswego County Health Association added a seventh week to its camp. When it launched its Christmas Seal campaign, the Association included details of the amount of food consumed by hungry children: campers gobbled up seventy quarts of milk and thirty-two loaves of bread each day. Seals revenue would also address maintenance challenges: the camp's well, only a few years old, could not keep up with supply demands and needed to be redrilled, and the staff recommended clearing the swamp behind the building for additional recreational space.

To avoid the Health Association and camp staff getting discouraged, Chairperson LeRoy Hollis offered some heartening medical news. A 50 percent drop in the number of Oswego County TB deaths was, according to the doctor, "mainly due to the facilities furnished for detection of cases and treatment at the Oswego County Sanatorium [and] better treatments and diagnosis, segregation of open cases and the work by county health nurses at locations like the Health Camp." To emphasize the importance of providing at-risk children with preventative measures, Hollis explained the latest scientific thinking behind the search for a TB cure:

> *It is generally considered that the majority of children have been exposed to tuberculosis by the time they have reached 10 or 12 years of age.* * *When the*

---

* This may have accounted for the Health Camp's downward shift in the average age of campers, which, by 1933, was six to ten years old.

tubercle bacilli enters the body of a normal individual for the first time and finds lodgement there, the number of bacilli may be so few and the normal resistance of the individual sufficient to effectively wall off the tubercle bacilli taken in, and no evidence of the disease develops. [However], the seed has been planted and unless the normal resistance of the body is kept up [author's emphasis], *the tubercle bacilli may commence to grow and multiply, infecting the tissues of the body where further tuberculosis processes may take place.*

Those cautionary words and the philanthropic nature of Oswego County residents kept the camp open, even as it faced new expenses. In 1934, just as the summer program was about to begin, the Health Association was forced to add another $420 to its financial responsibilities. The extra money was needed to purchase blankets for camper beds, which had previously been loaned from the National Guard. Again, a member of the Association suggested a unique solution: Bunco parties. Held throughout the county, each card-playing group wagered enough funds to buy one bed cover, building a new stack of blankets one at a time.

Leading the camp for her fourth year was Martha Foot, who oversaw the care of sixty-eight children that summer. One of her campers was my father, Silvio T. Farfaglia. Although Dad wasn't normally an expressive man, I remember hearing how much he loved going to the Health Camp. When each of his four children became age-eligible to attend Camp Hollis, Dad insisted we give it a try. When I began overseeing the Hollis facility, he talked more openly about his experiences there, and shortly before he died, he had them typed up. I've titled his Health Camp memories with a phrase he often used to sum up his summers at Lewis's Bluff:

"THEY TREATED US CAMPERS LIKE KINGS AND QUEENS"
I was eight years old when I first went to the Health Camp. It was for children at risk of disease and I always was a skinny child and sick a lot of the time. When a neighbor of ours told my parents about the camp, they signed me up.

Mom and Dad loaded me and my suitcase into their 1929 Model A Ford and drove to camp. I was going to stay for eight weeks! Except for weekly Sunday visits from my parents I was on my own for the summer! It was the first time I ever left home alone.

I remember being pretty nervous when I got there. I didn't know anyone, but the first thing I knew, I was in the middle of a dodgeball game. I guess

I played okay because after that I was accepted. From that point on, I knew I would be okay.

I learned so much while at Camp. Things we take for granted now, like taking a shower, were brand new to me. Back home we always took a bath in a round tub! I learned how to make my own bed at camp and at times would help wash and dry the dishes.

Like all the campers, Dad loved the meals, especially the ice-cold milk. And whenever he needed cooling off, there was the lake:

Boys and girls swam at separate times. We had a lot of fun diving off a big boulder about 25 feet from shore. I also learned to row camp's big old wooden boat.

I never had trouble falling asleep at camp. The waves hitting the shore was such a peaceful sound. To this day, if I have trouble falling asleep I try to think back to the sound of those waves on the shore.

I can't say enough about the counselors we had. I don't remember most of their names, but they all made a big impression on me. They had a way of making me feel at ease, of making me feel special. Of course, while they were doing that for me, they were doing that for all the other campers, too. One counselor, Ed, visited me a couple times at my house and that made me feel really cared about.

When I think back on my childhood I know I didn't participate much in school, but for some reason I did at camp. Maybe it was all the attention I got there that I just couldn't get back home and at school. Parents and teachers are so busy…

I was given the award of best camper, which was a great honor. They gave me a prize of a model airplane, which was very special to me. I also got an award for "most unique" rock. I can still see that rock's coloring in my mind.

I hated leaving the camp, even after eight weeks.

While my father was enjoying his Health Camp summers, the threat of tuberculosis was probably the furthest thing from his mind. But it remained a grave concern for those providing Dad and the other campers such a pleasurable experience. Despite advancements in the understanding and efforts to eradicate TB, reports showed it to be the greatest cause of death among children from infancy to age twenty. The Oswego County Health Camp still had much to achieve.

The 1936 season was exceptional only because Martha Foot stepped down from her leadership position, to be replaced by Mrs. A.D. Lewen, of Syracuse. The camp enjoyed another successful six-week program, serving seventy children. Mrs. Lewen would also be dealing with ongoing operational issues, like the need for the new sewage disposal system required by New York State's Health Department. It was the latest facility challenge for the camp, and after nine seasons at Lewis's Bluff, the Health Association began to see why maintenance problems seemed never-ending: they'd chosen to build their camp on a Lake Ontario bluff.

As picturesque as the views of Lake Ontario are, the camp's location near its shoreline had proven to be troublesome. A brief geology lesson explains why. Ontario's bluffs were formed by a receding glacier during the Ice Age. They started out as a single towering drumlin, an elongated hill made up of mud, clay, sand and small rocks left behind by the glacier. Centuries of lake storms' crashing waves and sustained winds ate away at that drumlin, removing a foot or more each year. What was left were standalone bluffs, and when Lewis's became home to the Health Camp and then Camp Hollis, its summer residents added to the erosion problem. In the camp's early history, the staff cleared an acre or so of land each summer to use for large group

Construction of the camp's original main building on a Lake Ontario bluff made for a beautiful view, but it also gave camp administrators a few headaches. *Courtesy of the Sullivan family.*

activities, removing mature vegetation with strong root systems and replacing them with lawn grass. At an ever-accelerating rate, erosion made drilling for potable water, maintaining a reliable septic system and protecting the main building a continuous battle.

To address these and other camp expenses, Dr. Hollis took his fundraising message to local service clubs. At the conclusion of the 1937 season (seventy-five children were served, with their weight gains ranging from two to nine pounds), the Fulton Rotary Club responded to Hollis's appeal for $7,000 to operate the Health Camp by voting to move their support from the Syracuse-based Fresh Air Camp Fund to Lewis's Bluff. Oswego's Kiwanis Club heard a similar message from Dr. Hollis, who shared his request as a parable:

> *We feel sorry for these underprivileged and undernourished children who do not have a good chance for health. But we cannot help by mere sympathy. Like the Good Samaritan, we must put our hands in our pocket and help them with financial aid.*

The doctor left Kiwanis members with an alarming statistic: 150 Oswego County children—twice the number the camp could accommodate—had "tuberculosis tendencies."

The Oswego Rotary Club responded to Dr. Hollis's message by pledging funds for the construction of a screened-in porch off the girls' dormitory. By 1938, campers and staff were enjoying an indoor setting on rainy days, but a new problem in the kitchen threatened their summer fun. The camp's refrigeration unit had given out. Of all the concerns the Health Association had, interruptions in meal preparation were to be avoided at all costs. Providing children healthy and plentiful food remained critical to the camp's success, and with menus now being planned by Cornell University's Department of Home Economics, it was one of the proudest accomplishments the Health Camp could claim. Again, Dr. Hollis made the fundraising rounds, looking for the dollars to purchase an eighty-by-seven-foot electric cooler room.

Continuing into the 1940s, the number of children served remained between sixty and seventy each summer. Appeals to purchase Christmas Seals continued, but the Health Association could not deny that sales were again decreasing. No one doubted that there was still work to be done in the fight to defeat tuberculosis, but medical efforts locally and across our nation had been overshadowed by an even bigger battle unfurling on the other side of the Atlantic Ocean: the United States was about to enter World War II.

The Oswego County Health Camp, like all organizations dependent on the charity of others, felt the impact of the war. In order to continue operating in 1942, the camp reduced its program to five weeks and served thirty-six children, about half its normal total. Then came this 1943 headline, confirming what many had feared: "Health Group Undecided on Camp Operation." The burden of determining whether to remain open or closed was placed on the shoulders of the Oswego County Health Association board, many of whom had worked to make the camp possible since its inception fifteen years ago: John C. Henry, Mrs. John Parsons and Miss Lucy Vincent, of Oswego; L.W. Emerick of Fulton; and their leader from Sandy Creek, Dr. LeRoy Hollis. Joining them would be a new board member, one whose surname foreshadowed the future of the county's beloved camp: from the city of Fulton, Mrs. Eugene (Ruth) Sullivan.

Sullivan and her fellow Health Association board members quickly learned the obstacles they faced to keep the camp afloat during the war years. Despite 1943 media's annual appeal for Christmas Seal purchases—the Oswego County Health Camp was notably missing from its list of beneficiaries—*and* the continued loss of life from tuberculosis, the Association's finances painted a grim picture. One reporter spelled it out: "The grand total of contemplated expenditures amounting to $3,123 does not make provision for the maintaining of the Children's Health Camp in 1943."

But the Association was not ready to give up. It passed a resolution authorizing its president, John Henry, to appoint a committee to "investigate the matter of operating the camp this year." The committee's task was to find a way to stretch its dollars, making every penny count. It made a noble attempt, but in July 1943, the Association's final decision was announced. That summer, the first since 1928, Oswego County would be unable to provide a healthy respite for its children in need. The report stated the reason, although no one needed to be reminded: "War restrictions on gasoline and other essentials for the camp."

In the summer of 1943, and the two that followed, Lewis's Bluff stood silent. Its buildings were boarded up, and the sounds of happy, healthy children were notably absent.

A JUDGE REIMAGINES
THE DREAM

I t's not that Oswego County officials abandoned the Health Camp, at least in their best intentions. While the county's cities, towns and rural communities worked together to support our nation's war efforts, those trying to eradicate tuberculosis kept their battle in the public's eye. A May 1945 *Mexico Independent* article had hopeful words for the Health Association's camp: "[Christmas Seals] alone finance the work of the Association which includes the maintenance, in peace times, of the children's health camp at Lewis's Bluff."

Peace did return to the world, and local priorities could once again turn to the needs of Oswego County's underprivileged children. One acutely aware of those needs was Fultonian Eugene F. Sullivan, who'd been following the success and unfortunate demise of the camp through his wife Ruth's membership on the Health Association's board. Eugene was not a native Fultonian, but it became his adopted hometown in his youth. New York City–born, he made frequent visits to Fulton, where his father, Richard, grew up. As owner of the Hotel Fulton, Richard and his family spent summers running the establishment, and by Eugene's high school years, the Sullivans had moved to the Oswego County city. After graduating from Albany Law School, where he met Ruth, the couple settled in Fulton.

Along with his legal practice, Sullivan was appointed to a position in 1944 that put him face to face with the realities of disadvantaged children. In his new role as Oswego County Children's Court judge, Eugene presided over Saturday morning sessions, where he met children who had been abandoned

Judge Eugene Sullivan presided over Oswego County's Children's Court, introducing him to boys and girls he believed could benefit from a recreational camp. *Courtesy of the Sullivan family.*

by their parents or who found themselves on the wrong side of the law. By 1946, he'd seen nearly three hundred such cases. Eugene's son Mike Sullivan (1952, 1955–57) described how those youngsters' ill-fated circumstances influenced his father's thinking:

> *Dad oversaw cases involving families who didn't even have the basic necessities. Things like running water for bathing or fresh milk for meals. My father thought those children needed something special in their lives. He'd say, "If we can give a kid something that they will enjoy, they will carry it with them and maybe we can cut down on the delinquency."*

At a 1940s Mexico Men's Club meeting, the judge explained how he developed this philosophy:

> *I haven't seen a bad boy or girl before me yet. Every single one of them are well worth saving. Our court is not a place where boys and girls are punished. It is, in fact and in practice, a place where conditions that would destroy boys and girls are corrected through the cooperation of the court.*

At first, Sullivan wasn't specifically thinking of a summer camp for those troubled children. But the idea of a recreational program began to formulate from something he'd observed in his own family. One of the activities his four children enjoyed was Scouting. Eugene's daughter Jane Ann Sullivan Spellman recalled that "as youngsters, my sister Sheila and I would do anything to be able to attend Girl Scout camp. Daddy saw how much we enjoyed it and was impressed with the skills my sister and I learned. He wanted all children to have that opportunity."

Having observed his children's enjoyment of camp, Sullivan began imagining how such a program might help the boys and girls in his court system. He kept thinking of the dormant campgrounds on Lewis's Bluff, but the thought of raising the money necessary to restart it seemed daunting. It was Ruth Sullivan who shared a possible solution to that financial roadblock.

Along with her parental responsibilities, Ruth worked outside the home, serving as legal counsel to New York state senators Isaac Mitchell and Henry A. Wise. She also maintained membership with a statewide organization known as the Republican Women of the Legislature. (She would serve as its president in 1948.) Commuting to Albany, the state's capital, on a weekly basis, Ruth received hot-off-the-press updates on newly enacted laws, including an innovative program sponsored by Governor Thomas E. Dewey. The governor's law, Ruth pointed out to her husband, was aimed at helping at-risk children, specifically juvenile delinquents.

By 1944, as World War II continued to consume the energy and resources of our country, New York State officials were noticing an uptick in youthful offenses. Blame for the rise was attributed to fathers fighting overseas and mothers working outside the home. Governor Dewey created a committee to study this dilemma, which led to the establishment of New York State's Youth Commission. Composed of representatives from its Departments of Correction, Education, Health, Mental Hygiene and Social Welfare, the commission developed a plan to reduce the number of youthful offenders.

When Judge Sullivan read the first law adopted at the recommendation of the commission, he found hope for resurrecting the Health Camp. In part, Chapter 556 of the Laws of 1945 authorized "the establishment, operation and maintenance of youth bureaus, recreation projects and education projects for the development, protection and security of children." Sullivan carefully studied the five-page law, noting what it defined as recreation projects: "A structure, property, interest, or activity owned, maintained or operated by or under the direction of a municipality, devoted in whole or in part to the provision of leisure-time activities for youth." That definition was just what Sullivan was looking for. To him, it described the abandoned camp at Lewis's Bluff, and one more section of the law suggested how he might go about resurrecting it (emphasis added): "The commission shall have the power and it shall be the duty of the commission to authorize and require, in accordance with the provisions of this act, *the payment of state aid to municipalities*."

Sullivan read on to learn more about this proposed aid. The state was offering up to a 50 percent reimbursement for the expenses of an approved youth project—half of what he would need to reopen the Lewis's Bluff camp. Soon, both Sullivans were serving on the Health Association's board and participating in robust debates about the pros and cons of running a camp. Judge Sullivan led those discussions whenever possible, but his private practice and Children's Court responsibilities sometimes conflicted with meeting dates. He missed one meeting during which the Association determined reopening the camp to be fiscally unwise. After he learned of the decision, at the subsequent meeting, a reporter captured the Judge's reaction:

> *With the fanaticism of one dedicated to a hallowed cause,* [Sullivan] *took the floor. Did his listeners know, he demanded, the hundreds of area children who were forced to spend their summers in the confines of their home communities because of a dearth of available camps? Were they aware of the healthful influence—both physical and moral—a few days in the open could exert on the county's youth? Were they?*

Those were strong words indeed, but they were spoken by a man whose duties showed him, again and again, why the Health Association should reconsider its decision. Committee members responded with an offer: if Sullivan thought he had an idea worth fighting for, they would support him. As the reporter concluded, "The judge suddenly found himself with the camp in his hands."

Sullivan didn't waste any time thanking the Association—in fact, he didn't have much time. It was late fall of 1945 when it had given him the green light, and the judge intended to have his camp ready for children by the beginning of the next summer.

The first major hurdle, if Sullivan and the Health Association wanted to realize a 50 percent reimbursement from the state, was to place the camp under ownership, maintenance or operation of a municipality. Using his ties to Oswego County through its Children's Court, the judge asked its Board of Supervisors to consider overseeing the camp. As autumn gave way to winter, Sullivan spoke at board committee meetings and shared his vision one-on-one with supervisors, informing them of the potential state funding that could breathe new life into the vacant camp. The board's biggest question was why, with its many obligations to county residents, it should add the operation of a children's camp? Judge made his case by connecting the dots. A lack of healthy recreational activities, he explained, breeds juvenile delinquency.

Once the judge gained support from a few supervisors, he asked if they might arrange for him to speak to the full board. Although he was promised the opportunity, county business kept bumping his camp off the meeting agendas, and as the date of camp's proposed opening approached, Sullivan knew that he had to move forward. In June 1946, the Health Association appointed a committee to prepare for the Health Camp's reopening. Sullivan was named its chairman, with E.M. Waterbury, R.W. Allison, John Henry, H.H. Stevens, Mrs. Charles Morris, Miss Lucy Vincent, Miss Aura Cole and Mrs. A.C. Parker as members. One additional association member was already quite familiar with preparing a summer camp: Dr. LeRoy Hollis.

While the committee began putting the puzzle pieces of a summer camp together, the Board of Supervisors finally agreed to host Sullivan at its next regularly scheduled meeting in late July, too late for Sullivan's proposed opening date. A special session was called, with every supervisor expected to be in attendance. On July 2, all twenty-seven members of the board were in the county chambers to hear Clerk William Algan state the purpose of the meeting: "To take action on any resolutions that may be presented for the purpose of establishing a Youth Agency in the county as provided by Chapter 556 of the Laws of 1945."

The floor was then ceded to Judge Sullivan, who explained his proposed camp project. Joining him were H.H. Stevens, who'd previously directed a health camp, and Kenneth Miller, Oswego County 4-H agent. Sullivan then introduced James T. Cosgrove, from the New York State Youth Commission, who explained the potential state funding and answered the supervisors' questions. Discussion followed, with Supervisor Fred Haynes, of Oswego Town, eventually calling for a resolution, which read in part:

> *Whereas it is the intention of the County of Oswego to establish a Recreation and Education Project, and*
>
> *Whereas, the County of Oswego is about to submit an application for such project to the New York State Youth Commission…*
>
> *Be it resolved that such application is in all respects approved and the Chairman of this Board is hereby directed and authorized to duly execute said application and forward it to the New York State Youth Commission for its approval.*

Sullivan was particularly happy with the board's next decision: "This resolution shall take effect immediately." All twenty-seven supervisors cast their ayes.

The good news traveled fast, with the *Pulaski Democrat* among the first newspapers to report that the State of New York had given Sullivan's camp its stamp of approval. Its headline stated, "County Health Camp to Receive Aid Under Youth Program":

> *County Judge Eugene F. Sullivan…has been advised by Robert Kates, of the New York State Youth Commission, that the Commission has approved the Oswego County Health Camp for participation in state aid under the Youth program. This means the state will share in the cost of the camp operation, reimbursing one-half of the total of most expenditures.*

Not only was Mr. Kates's pledge a solid support of the camp, but it was also groundbreaking for New York State youth. As Kates made sure to note, "The Oswego County project is the first of this type to be given the approval of the Commission. The Commission would regard the local project as an experiment and if it worked out satisfactorily, another year's approval would be given by the Commission." Who, reading those words in 1946, could have foreseen that Sullivan's "experiment" on Lewis's Bluff would one day be considered a pioneering model for youth advocacy?

But there was no time to celebrate. While the Health Association continued to work on building repair, program development and camper recruitment, the judge's major task was to secure the other half of moneys needed to operate his camp. Adding to this responsibility was the fact that he would not be seeking funding for a typical summer camp, like the ones his children enjoyed through Scouting or that other youngsters attended through their church or local YMCA. Sullivan's camp would be financially unique in two ways.

First, though fully intending to serve the underprivileged and unfortunate, Sullivan's vision was more inclusive. His camp would welcome any Oswego County child who was not able to attend another camp. Second, a child's participation at the camp would come without any cost to his or her family. The judge's stipulations, though worthy, added more pressure on those who were fundraising for him. Health Association member Mrs. John Parsons expanded her Christmas Seal sales promotion, and community leaders wrote editorials praising the former Lewis's Bluff camp. Dr. Hollis, seventy-five years old but energized by his Health Camp's possible rejuvenation, spoke on behalf of the new program.

But spearheading it all was Sullivan. He made speeches at service organizations, school boards, churches and town halls—anywhere people might support his belief that a child's life could be enriched from a summer camp vacation. Pledges for his proposal were announced through local media, with the announcement of "up to $3,000 towards the cost of operating the camp this year." More good news came from the county's Board of Supervisors: its annual budget included a line item for $1,869.56 toward "the Oswego County Health Camp." Finally, with Sullivan's camp on firmer, if not solid, ground, the judge could turn his attention to its program.

Margaret Sullivan, an RN from Fulton, took charge of nursing services. Lucy Vincent, a second RN, from Oswego, would select the children to attend camp. Robert Allison, president of the Wilcox Brothers Grocers, was to handle food and supplies. Oswegonians Mary Kehoe Morris and Robert L. Allison assumed responsibility for the camp's property and insurance. E.M. Waterbury, of Oswego's *Palladium-Times*, guaranteed plenty of publicity for the camp. Making sure it all came together was Virginia Simons, the Health Association's executive secretary.

Next, Sullivan addressed the camp's building and grounds issues. A health inspector recommended an updated hot water system (including a state-of-the-art "regulating jack" to control water temperature) and upgrades on the camp's well. When it looked like repairs to the well would not be made in time for camp's opening date, the decision was made to haul water to the site in ten-gallon milk cans. The kitchen's two stoves were fired up, and an eight-by-ten-foot cold storage unit was added. The Health Association claimed bragging rights about its modern refrigerated unit, which it noted could accommodate "all the fruits and vegetables hungry campers could consume and a full carcass."

Everywhere the judge looked—from the bottom of the well to the treetops on an overgrown playground—there was more to be done. "I don't know how Dad was able to pull off getting that camp open," Judge's son Mike reflected many years later. Mike can still list the vendors who answered Sullivan's call for help in those first tenuous years. There was Harvey Laskey, who owned Netherland's Dairy ("We'd get that milk in large cans and scoop it out with ladles into the children's cups"); Wilcox Brothers, run by Bob Allison, which delivered food from its East First Street Oswego location; Neil O'Brien ("They provided us with lumber and hardware"); and a carpenter named Felice Pompey, who used those construction supplies to patch holes and secure the main building. And who from

Judge Sullivan's Notes: "How to Start a Summer Camp."

those early years could forget Frank "Dynamite" Gould, owner of a bus company? ("He took old buses and refurbished them, and that's how lots of kids got to camp week after week.")

Next, Judge turned his attention to those who would devote their summer to providing children fun and guidance. Through his frequent contact with school personnel, Sullivan found a camp director in Herman H. (also known as H.H.) Stevens, principal of the Minetto Union Free Academy. According to the judge's daughter Jane, her father admired the educational philosophies of Stevens, who was a frequent speaker at Oswego County teachers' conferences. When Sullivan was preparing his camp, Stevens was working toward a doctorate degree in outdoor education. It was a win-win: Stevens could collect data for his doctoral paper, "The Personality Changes that Take Place During a Camping Period," and Sullivan had a forward-thinking leader for his new camp.

Stevens was then given what is perhaps a camp director's most important job: building a staff that would serve as enthusiastic role models for children. H.H. found six young adults whose résumés confirmed their abilities: Alan Ranous had recently completed three years in the army and was an assistant scoutmaster; Clarence McKinstry, due to begin Oswego State Teachers College in the fall, was active in several sports; Helen Longway, a student at the college, was president of the Girls Athletic Association; Eunice Nichols, set to begin teaching that fall, was also a member of the Athletic Association and the college's mixed choir; her brother, Kenneth Nichols, had been accepted into the college's physical education program; and Norma Clark, a sophomore at the college, had attended a counselor training program, where she earned her aquatic lifesaving certificate.

With Stevens and his staff in place, the judge worked with them to plan the six weeks of camp's inaugural season, settling on two three-week sessions: one for children ages six to nine and the second for children ten to thirteen. Sullivan then began spreading the word about his camp through schools, townships and medical facilities. But the judge had to look no further than his courtroom to find worthy candidates. When he met a child who'd gotten in trouble or came from a needful family, he'd mention the camp to the parent.

There was another group of children Sullivan wanted at his camp: boys and girls who found themselves in front of his judicial bench through no fault of their own. Those youngsters were abandoned and had no place to turn but an Oswego County orphanage, and by 1946, of the 125 children the county deemed in need of support, 77 were removed from homes and institutionalized. The judge established relationships with Oswego's two orphanages: St. Francis' Home, located on the city's east side (where Bishop Commons now stands), and the Oswego Children's Home, situated on the west side's Ellen Street. Keenly aware of what orphanages were able to provide and what they oftentimes lacked, the judge had a thought: Wouldn't a respite from life in a residential facility be just what those children needed?

Hundreds of boys and girls from those Oswego orphanages eventually benefited from Sullivan's belief. From the very first summer of his camp, they were at the top of registration's priority list. And there was no mistaking them when they arrived at camp. Carrying a paper sack—their "suitcase" for a three-week stay—they'd been sent with a pair of jeans, shorts (which would double as a bathing suit), a few changes of socks and underwear and several striped T-shirts. Decades later, when I reviewed photographs of the camp's early years, I had no idea why so many children wore those striped shirts. It was only in recent years that I learned the reason.

In the summer of 2009, Camp Hollis received a visit from the Fisher brothers, Frank and Craig, who grew up in an Oswego orphanage. They'd traveled from out of state to visit the city that raised them and made sure to include a stop at the camp where some of their happiest childhood memories were made. Frank, who explained that those striped T-shirts were part of the uniform the orphanage provided for youngsters, has written a book about his experiences as an orphan. In his introduction, he wrote:

The Oswego Orphan Asylum, later renamed the Oswego Children's Home, became my home within days of my ninth birthday in January 1951. Our caregiver grandmother died January 14, 1951. And soon thereafter we were placed, as our parents' legal separation became effective and neither took any of us. [Along with Craig, Frank had three other siblings who were placed in the home.] *During those years, thousands of children were served by comparatively few employees. Oswego County switched over to Foster Care for kids and closed the Home in the summer of 1956. I was at Camp Hollis when it closed.*

Children enjoying playtime during one of Camp Hollis's first seasons; those in striped T-shirts were from local orphanages. *Courtesy of the Sullivan family.*

Frank has vivid memories of the contrast between his five and a half years at the Home and his brief vacations at Camp Hollis:

> *Boys and girls were kept separated in the home....It was very sad that we didn't get to be with our younger sister. She was only six and suddenly alone after having been in a family with three older brothers. The overnight Camp Hollis experience was clearly better than the Children's Home because Hollis counselors participated in activities with the children and cared that they had a good experience.*

One of the counselors who noticed campers in need was Pat McConnell Pritchard (1948–52). When Camp Hollis celebrated its fiftieth anniversary, Pat offered this memory of children from the orphanages: "Many were starved for love. You could put your arm around them and hug them. They needed lots of love and they got it at Camp Hollis."

During one of the years Frank attended Camp Hollis, 1955, twelve of the thirty-five children living at the Home were able to attend Camp Hollis. Among them was William Dickerson, who remembered how different it was to be staying at the Camp Hollis boys' dorm:

> [At both the orphanage and camp] *we were versed in good order, but the big difference is the order at the Home was overseen by a rather stern, humorless woman who slept in a private room just off the dormitory and woke us up by slapping her slipper on the wall and yelling, "Rise and shine!" At the camp it was college students who were a lot more fun, even when they were pretending to be strict.*

Frank's brother Craig needed only a few words to express what it meant for him to be one of the lucky orphans who went to camp: "It was the highlight of the year—by far. At the end of my stay, as we got on the bus to go back to the Children's Home, I literally cried. It was so oppressive to go back to the 'Home.'"

Frank and Craig's younger sister, Christine, was one of the children at the Home waiting for her turn to attend Camp Hollis: "I remember other girls coming back looking like bright new pennies with happy faces and excitement vibrating behind their eyes." It took a few years, but once Christine got her chance to step off the bus onto the campgrounds, she was ready. Nearly seventy years later, she shared in great detail what being a Camp Hollis camper meant:

> *We were gathered around counselors and checked into the dormitory. Cots were lined up head to foot along two walls and a few cots went down the middle aisle. My cot, as all, had clean sheets and an army blanket. Nailed to the wall above the cot was a wooden structure, like an old milk crate, with two open shelves for our things.*
>
> *We unpacked our few belongings amid shouts between friends and quick introductions to those close by. Counselors came to show us what we needed to know, like where the bathroom was. We lined up for the dining room and then had a simple lunch. The tables were set up in long rows with chairs on each side. We were taught how to bus our space. Lunch was followed by counselors going over our schedules so we knew when we could go to the lake or games or crafts or simply run free in fields and grounds.*

Christine Fisher, who attended Hollis while living in the Oswego Children's Home, described her camp experience as "a whole new world." *Courtesy of the Fisher family.*

Christine spoke for many when she wrote those memories, especially in how she chose to end her story, which reads like the ultimate compliment to Judge Sullivan's belief that a few weeks of summer fun could make a difference in a child's life: "I went to Camp Hollis for three more years," Christine happily reported.

Getting the chance to go to Camp Hollis has been the hope of children since its first campers arrived on the morning of July 8, 1946. Twenty-seven girls and as many boys were selected from orphanages and recommendations by school nurses, probation workers, police officers and county social servants. On their way to claim a cot in the dormitories, the excited youngsters passed a humble playground of six swings, a maypole and a foot-propelled miniature merry-go-round. In the distance, they saw a trail heading into the woods and Lake Ontario's welcoming blue waters. A counselor talked up the special events staff had planned: a hot dog roast on the beach, a refreshing dip in the lake and an overnight hike for boys at the nearby Salvadore's Grove.

Before the fun could begin, there were a few things to address. The mandatory health check included, if needed, a shower and haircut. A scale located just outside the nurse's office continued the Health Camp's practice of monitoring children's weight.[*] Then the children were escorted to the dining hall, where they were served food—and plenty of it. Mrs. Hilda Brown, of Fruit Valley, was a good choice for kitchen manager; she'd previously fed crowds at the Fort Ontario Officers Club. A feature news story listed what she had planned for hungry children: "Breakfast on Monday consisted of fruit juice, oatmeal, bread and butter, with dinner comprising beef stew, vegetables and cupcakes. Supper brought vegetable salad, peaches, and more bread and butter." There were special foods on certain days. "Fish is on Friday and ice cream added to the dinner menu

---

[*] Keeping track of campers' health improvements continued into the 1960s; registration cards from that era included a space to record a child's start and end weight.

on Sunday." Milk, of course, was on the menu, but it wasn't measured in glassfuls. "Each child," the reporter noted, "has approximately one and one-half quarts of milk a day."

Judge Sullivan knew that nutritious meals were an important part of his new camp, and he wanted to make sure those contributing funds could witness the children's hearty appetites. In a letter to the chairman of the New York State Youth Commission, the judge invited him to visit camp. "Arrive by lunch," he wrote, "so you can see the kids eat."

Along with nutritious meals and healthy physical activities, Sullivan made sure that campers were exposed to Christian values. A devout Catholic, he believed that a religious program would be important for those who may not have had the opportunity back home. Mike Sullivan remembered that "Dad came every Sunday with his big car and took the Catholic children to a chapel at the sharp curve on Snake Swamp Road. Monsignor Quade would come from St. Mary's Church in Oswego to give Mass. Sometimes Dad had to make three or four trips to get that many children to the chapel."

The judge's practice of getting all Catholics to Mass would continue for many years, with Oswego's Knights of Columbus also furnishing transportation to church for children. Girls of Catholic faith were expected to bring a dress from home, and if they didn't have a hat, counselors improvised with a handkerchief to cover their heads. One of those counselors was my sister, Chris Farfaglia Goebert (1969, 1971–72). Chris hasn't forgotten what Sunday mornings at the camp meant:

> *I remember riding to church in the front seat of Judge Sullivan's Cadillac. The car seemed huge, like the judge, even to me as a counselor. One Sunday, I decided I was going to skip church and stay back at camp, but the judge wouldn't hear of it. He sent someone into the girl counselors' quarters and insisted I get dressed for church and be outside in five minutes. Needless to say, I hurried and got dressed—and never skipped church again.*

Sullivan also made provisions for campers who were not Catholic. "Dad befriended Reverend John Scarlett," Mike explained, "who came on Sundays to lead a Presbyterian service." In later years, the Oswego Ministerial Association supplied a clergyman each Sunday afternoon to conduct services at the camp for Protestant children. Camper William Dickerson remembered riding from camp to the Southwest Oswego Baptist Church.

The judge was involved with every aspect of the camp. His son Mike, though only nine years old when his father started the camp, paid attention to what that entailed:

> *I rode out with my father when he went to camp* [to check on its progress] *and it was my job to make sure he did not fall asleep on the way home. This was at least three nights a week. I also remember attending dinners where Dad gave the Camp Hollis pitch for funding. Money ran out the last two weeks of that first summer and Dad personally covered the paychecks for everyone.*

Prior to the camp's reopening and during its first three-week session, Sullivan and the County Health Association were still referring to their new program by its previous name, the Oswego County Health Camp. But soon after, they had reason to suggest a name change. On July 13, 1946, while the first group of children enjoyed the rejuvenated camp on Lewis's Bluff, Dr. Hollis died. News spread countywide, including this decision: "After the death of Dr. LeRoy F. Hollis, of Lacona, who had been a moving spirit in establishment of the Health Camp, [the Association voted] to name the camp in his honor."

By opening day of its second summer, a wooden sign was swinging from a post at the road into camp, linking its proud past to a promising future:

Camp Hollis
Children's Health Camp, Oswego County Health Association

A CAMP FOR ALL CHILDREN

Having survived its inaugural summer and with the camp aptly renamed, the Health Association made a few changes for its second season. Sullivan, well aware of his growing list of children eager to attend camp, proposed trimming the three-week sessions down to two weeks, thus adding an additional session and allowing sixty more children to move from waiting list to summer fun. To further trim the list, Sullivan offered a second idea: a day camp that would run concurrently with overnight sessions.

Soon, at high schools throughout the county, a line of children would form each weekday summer morning, waiting for a bus. In their hand was a small piece of paper with a handwritten note: "For Day Camp. Admit to Bus for Camp Hollis." It was signed "J.S.," Judge Sullivan. As many as fifty children traveled to the camp each day, enjoying nonstop activities, a refreshing dip in the lake and a sandwich lunch. There was a rotating schedule to accommodate as many children as possible: Wednesdays were set aside for Fulton youth, Oswego kids got Tuesdays and Thursdays and the remainder of the county's boys and girls enjoyed Mondays and Fridays.

Of course, those attending day camp wanted their chance to stay overnight, further expanding the waiting list. So did Sullivan's pledge to invite *all* children who did not have another opportunity to attend summer camp. The county's Board of Supervisors was asked to recruit youngsters from its towns and rural areas. Parents learned that they could call their county representative to be put on the list. This cross-section of children gave Camp Hollis a unique aspect that continues today: children from all walks of life are bunked together, learning to function as a unified group.

By the conclusion of 1947's summer season, those changes more than doubled the number of youth served by Camp Hollis to 273. Included in that increase were 54 boys and girls from the Children's Home, 12 from St. Francis Home, 36 from 4-H Clubs, 59 day and overnight campers from Fulton, 66 day and overnight campers from Oswego, 21 campers from other Oswego County towns and 25 boys who were guests of a special end-of-summer camp sponsored by the Oswego and Fulton Police Departments.

Other numbers covered in the Health Association's 1947 report can be found in paperwork from Camp Hollis's early history. Long rolls of adding machine tape listed numbers big and small: the camp's expenditures for the season. Their total of $7,343.76 covered capital improvements of $1,753.64 (including a slide and jungle bars for the playground); repairs, $270.30; salaries, $2,547.82; supplies, $2,156.66; incidentals, $242.60; and $58 to close the camp for the season. To help cover expenses, Oswego County's Board of Supervisors again called for a resolution to accept funds from the State of New York, pointing out that the county's revitalized health camp served "underprivileged and undernourished children." The State Youth Commission made good on its agreement to reimburse half of the total expenditures, $3,671.88.

Who covered the other half of Hollis's expenses? There was $2,500 from the New York State Committee on Tuberculosis and Public Health (through Christmas Seal sales) and $1,049.73 from Oswego County.[*] With 4-H Clubs' contribution of $306 and Fulton and Oswego Police Departments donating $200 each, it looked like Hollis ended 1947 with a $583.85 surplus. But Sullivan and his committee weren't able to bank that money. There was another financial obligation to satisfy: payment for the camp's insurance policy. Still, ending up with all bills paid was a good omen for the future of Camp Hollis. Unfortunately, the path of its success was about to hit a roadblock.

As planning for the 1948 camp season began, the Association received some disappointing news. Christmas Seal sales, the fiscal lifeblood of the Health Camp and a major contributor to Camp Hollis's first two seasons, were abruptly terminated. The reason, officials explained, had to do with major advances made in the fight against tuberculosis. The *Sandy Creek News* noted that "the program of X-ray surveys inaugurated this year in Oswego

---

[*] The county's contribution to the camp steadily grew. By 1952, it was a solid $7,000; it jumped to $12,000 in 1955; and by 1961, it covered $17,500 of Camp Hollis expenses. This strong support continues today. In 2019, Oswego County provided $140,000, or approximately 58 percent of the camp's budget.

County has proved very much more efficient and effective." In terms of modern medicine, health camps were no longer considered essential.

To address this loss of a major Hollis funder, the Health Association asked Oswego County to take a stronger role in overseeing the camp. The county obliged, as noted in its 1948 resolution, which "authorized the appointment of a committee to consist of the Chairman of the Board of Supervisors and four members thereof, to act in conjunction with the Camp Hollis Committee of Oswego County Health Association." In earnest, the new partnership began searching for additional funding. They found it in the Community Chest.

Established in 1913, the Chest provided a single charitable organization to support a community's needs. Its aid for our country's disadvantaged was firmly established during the Great Depression, and the number of Community Chest chapters across the United States had grown to nearly four hundred by the early 1940s.* In 1948, when Camp Hollis was struggling to secure sufficient funding, there were Community Chests in Oswego and Fulton. Both stepped up to support the camp.

Judge Sullivan knew that to build a solid foundation on which his camp could grow, the public must be made aware of it. And what better way to do so than a parade? Beginning in 1948, Sullivan tapped into the camp's Arts & Crafts staff to create a float for Oswego's Fourth of July celebration. Constructed on an Oswego Trucking Company flatbed, the float featured a large mural of the Hollis building. There were so many counselors and campers who wanted to participate in the parade that they marched alongside and behind the float, a sea of children wearing their official Camp Hollis T-shirts.

The T-shirt was another popular promotional idea from the judge. For years, he ordered dozens of camper and staff shirts, with instructions on the order form from the first year, 1948, requesting that "T-shirts were to be white with red lettering"; its now-legendary logo of four camp activities in a circle was "left to your best judgment." Sullivan's handwritten note on the paid receipt indicated that the Elks Lodges of Fulton and Oswego helped cover the cost. The T-shirts were an instant hit, and returning campers were reminded of it in their acceptance letter. Printed on official Hollis stationery, which listed thirteen agencies contributing to the camp, children were advised what to pack for their stay, ending with this phrase: "Wear Your Camp Hollis T-Shirt."

---

* During the Second World War, the Community Chest combined with the War Chest and then, in 1963, became known as the United Way.

Hollis's float in Oswego's Fourth of July celebration was both a crowd-pleaser and an exciting experience for campers marching in the parade. *Courtesy of the Sullivan family.*

The Hollis stationery was also used by Sullivan to invite the Board of Supervisors to a camp event: a summer cookout to thank county officials for their support of his recreational endeavor. The judge chose his words carefully, explaining that the picnic would take place "rain or shine, business or vacation, work or play, for or against, Republican or Democrat, male or female, town or city, young or…you're all young, unless you don't come."

Hollis's first picnic for county leaders was so enjoyable that it became an annual event that continues today. By the 1960s, the camp staff had created a special program for Oswego County officials to enjoy with their lunch. Following the meal, counselors and campers offered a song or two and maybe a skit. Ron Todd, a camper in that era, remembered a spoof featuring him and his twin brother, Don:

> *There were actually three sets of twins at camp during our session and our counselors put the six of us in a skit they called "Quick Change Artists." One of each set of twins would be in the kitchen. One by one, we'd walk through the dining hall fully dressed and then head to the boys dorm. Immediately, our twin would enter the dining hall—dressed in their bathing suits. It would have been a real crowd pleaser if one of the county guests hadn't known our family and gave away the secret!*

The Health Association's 1948 end-of-season financial report gave Hollis staff and county officials reason to celebrate. After managing again to balance its budget, the Association recommended the purchase of six more acres of land from neighbor Ben Place. The approved expansion, which allowed for a new baseball field and space for large group activities, was necessary.

Oswego County Legislators have been enjoying a picnic lunch at Camp Hollis for more than sixty years. *Courtesy of the Oswego County Office of Promotion & Tourism.*

Despite moving from three-week to two-week sessions and providing day camp programs, there were still 140 children whose summer did not include the Camp Hollis stay they'd hoped for.

That waiting list would continue year after year. Sullivan mentioned it in his October 1950 letter to the Lake City Police Club of Oswego, which had made a generous contribution. "The children had a most successful year at Camp Hollis and each child who attended expressed a desire to return in 1951." Of course, if every child wanting a second and third stay got their wish, there'd be little room for anyone else. Sullivan made a decision: the camp would start each summer offering a session to children who'd never been to Hollis before.

The number of satisfied campers grew. In 1952, 1,800 youngsters visited—300 as residential campers and the remainder in day and youth programs. In anticipation of its 1953 season, the Association made an unusual request to Oswego County officials. Would they consider shifting from a partnership with them to assuming full responsibility of the camp? The request had nothing to do with the growing number of unserved children. Something was threatening to happen on Lewis's Bluff, and if left unattended, it would mean disaster for Camp Hollis.

The concern was for the camp's main building. Not the quarter-century-old structure itself, but where it had been built. Set dramatically close to the bluff's swift drop to the Lake Ontario shore, the building gave visitors the feeling of being right on the water—so close, in fact, that former campers recall mist from the lake settling on them as they slept in the dorms. For a few years, its proximity to the lake added to the camp's charm, but as erosion ate away at the distance between the building and the drop-off, Camp Hollis was in the precarious position of tumbling into Lake Ontario.

The Health Association knew that something needed to be done and fast. With its expanded responsibilities beyond TB prevention, the Association was not in a position to supervise or finance building repairs. Was Oswego County? At the end of the 1953 camp season, the Association's president, Reverend Scarlett, put that question to the county's Board of Supervisors. They debated the request, with many voicing their concern that governmental bodies were not normally in the business of operating residential summer camps.* The county also had recently agreed to take responsibility for another health-related project: Dr. Hollis's Orwell Sanatorium. The pros and cons were discussed, with Supervisor John Mercier, from Oswego, declaring, "We can't throw out 2,000 kids!" That was a hard statement to dispute, and the board unanimously agreed to create a committee that would, along with the Health Association, determine the future of Camp Hollis.

One year later, on September 2, 1954, after another season of the camp sitting on eroding ground, the Board of Supervisors passed a resolution to create the Oswego County Recreation Commission. A second resolution immediately followed, appointing Judge Sullivan as the committee's chairman; Charles Sauers, of Phoenix, as its secretary; and Williamstown's Hugh Dowling and Oswego's Reverend Scarlett and Carl Richardson as committee members. A final third resolution of that meeting authorized the County of Oswego to take title of the camp. In a board-wide show of support, all three resolutions passed unanimously.

The responsibilities for the county's new Recreation Commission were announced. It would supervise the camp's summer director and staff. It would oversee expenditures, ensuring that the camp would stay within its allotted budget. And most urgently, it would address the issue of how to save the camp's building. Ideally, the commission would have called for a thorough review of the structure's integrity and the bluff's erosion problem. The members knew that construction experts should have been called in

---

* In fact, in my tenure associated with Camp Hollis, I only met one other director of a municipally sponsored residential camp.

for consultation. But there wasn't time for that. The Board of Supervisors suggested a speedier plan.

Since it was now part of Oswego County's governmental structure, Camp Hollis would have access to its many departments, including Public Works, which was responsible for hefty tasks like snowplowing and road construction. Couldn't the camp building be moved, one supervisor suggested, by Public Works' industrial-sized equipment? Certainly, it would be a difficult endeavor given the building's U-shaped design. But what if it were divided into three sections—the two dorms and the kitchen/dining hall—and moved piece by piece? The risky plan was approved, but only after the county recruited support from an organization not normally associated with summer camps: the U.S. Navy.

More specifically, it was the U.S. Navy Reserve's special division responsible for building projects, the Construction Battalion, or "CB." Better known as Seabees, the group's motto was just what Oswego County was looking for: "Anything we are tasked with, we can do." As proof, the Liverpool, New York Seabees, located in nearby Onondaga County, had already provided muscle for another camp, YMCA's Camp Tousey, which had a building in need of a facelift. When Oswego County told the Seabees of Camp Hollis's troubled shoreline structure, the battalion pledged its support.

As a team, Oswego County's Public Works and the Liverpool Seabees spent the fall of 1954 and winter of '55 planning for the move. By spring, on a site a few hundred yards inland from the bluff, they cleared an area and set the building's new foundations and footings. Then, in a single weekend, the only indoor space on the campgrounds was moved, in mammoth puzzle pieces, to its new home. In quick succession, a local mason patched the fireplace, which had suffered some damage during the move; the aging roof was replaced; and a new septic system was installed. All told, the project cost the county $20,000 ($191,000 today).

"We've been asked to move your whole building, but it might just be easier to move the whole lake."

Along with its move to a new location, Camp Hollis also moved into a new era. After Director H.H. Stevens oversaw the camp's first five seasons, new leaders spent a summer or two at the helm. Then, in 1956, Oswegonian Robert Bellinger, a

After years of battling bluff erosion, Camp Hollis's main building was moved several hundred yards inland. *Courtesy of Sarah Gould Hill.*

Liverpool Schools math teacher, began his five-year run as camp director. Along with operating Hollis from its new location, Bellinger also found himself in charge of a larger facility. After the county paid Ben and Helen Place $1,500 for another seven acres of land, the camp's property doubled.

According to Bellinger, the Places and Camp Hollis had a neighborly relationship. He recalled that Ben, who was the town of Oswego's justice of the peace, made frequent stops at the camp. "We built a screened-in porch behind the kitchen and kept the garbage there until Ben picked it up for his pigs."

Along with supervising a larger facility, Bob was responsible for other camp improvements. "We erected the flagpole, where we said the Pledge of Allegiance each morning." Camp also secured its own vehicle: a Plymouth station wagon that "we used to pick up supplies from several vendors." But perhaps most welcomed by the children was the "huge slide we could put in the water. It had to come out at the end of the day because you never knew when a storm would come up."

Sundays were special at the camp, according to Bob. After church services, "lunch was turkey from Lamb's Farm on Hall Road, and the day would end with a campfire and hot dog roast." Friday's supper was also noteworthy. "We'd celebrate with a fish fry from Cahill's." But more important than meals were the many events Bob and his staff planned for the kids:

> *I called Oswego Speedway and got the whole camp in for free. When the circus was in town, I was able to have the Shriners have our campers attend at no cost. Through Bob Burdick, we all went to the Scriba Firemen's Field Days for an evening of fun. One summer, one of our counselors got married and I made arrangements for "Dynamite" Gould to bus everyone to the church. We took up a whole section of St. Mary's.*

All of this was done in tight living quarters for the Bellingers: Bob, his wife and young child. "We had two small rooms; one of which was my office." Pay for his staff was just as sparse. "Counselors made $200 for ten weeks. As a consolation, camp arranged for them to have cube steaks and Cokes for their evening snack. Most evenings you could smell the steaks cooking in the kitchen."

Enjoying those evening snacks was one of Bob's counselors, Cindy Czerow Nacey (1957–58). Cindy was an Oswego College student and had seen an advertisement for the camp job. Since she was studying to be a teacher, she thought it would be good experience. She did learn a lot, Cindy recalled, but not in a conventional way. "There was really no staff training. The very first day, we girls washed all the windows and the guys came in on a big truck filled with mattresses. Also on that first day, we took lake stones and painted an American flag on the bluff, where it stayed the whole summer."[*]

Cindy taught the campers archery, although she admits she'd never been trained. Nor was she a lifeguard, but counselors were still expected to be on duty at the lake: "We had swimming every day and taught kids the basics, no matter what the weather was. On days when the water was rough, we counselors would make a line, arm in arm."

Hollis hikes in the 1950s were taken on a single trail. "It began at the bluff," Cindy explained, "and on the trail, we'd come to an old trailer, telling the kids that someone named 'The Hermit' lived there. 'Keep on the trail,' we'd warn them, 'or he might capture you.'" Rainy days, for Cindy and the staff, meant a movie "like *Cinderella*. Tables were pushed to the side and campers sat on lined up benches eating popcorn we'd made."

Food was, of course, plentiful. Cindy remembered "big bowls of vegetables that local farmers had donated." And after satisfying meals, there was singing: "The kids loved the song 'Amsterdam' because they could yell 'Dam!' at the end. They'd yell it so loud, it would raise the roof." Camper Linda Jessmore, who attended Hollis when Cindy was a counselor, also loved the musical ending to mealtimes. "We sang, 'If You're Happy and You Know It.' Boy, the floor in the dining hall would shake when we stomped our feet."

Cindy described the high health standards maintained at the camp, including shower day for the children. "It took place right before bedtime. There were only two showerheads in the girls' bathroom, so that was quite a chore getting 30 of them showered." There were bedroom rules for both campers *and* staff. "Counselors had a curfew of 10:00 p.m. We had to be in our staff rooms at that time—no exceptions."

---

[*] This activity was resurrected in 1976 to celebrate our nation's bicentennial. Campers formed a line and passed flat rocks from beach to bluff, where they were turned into red, white or blue stones shining under a Fourth of July sun.

A ten o'clock curfew seems strict for those teenage counselors, but they found ways to make their own fun, including an activity Cindy participated in that still takes place from time to time. "On the last day of camp, the counselors had a mud fight [later known as mud soccer] in a big puddle that always collected at the bottom of the dirt road that led to the main building. One summer I was wearing a white sweatshirt and it got completely muddied up. I think it was Pat Sullivan who carried me down to the lake and threw me in the water to get as cleaned off as I could before I went home."

Cindy was busy supervising lots of kids having all that fun. Another one of Bob Bellinger's camp improvements was his partnership with Fulton Recreation supervisor John Muscalino and Oswego Recreation director Roy (Mike) McCrobie. Bellinger invited their cities' youth for an expanded day camp, and by the end of the 1957 season—eleven years after the camp's first summer had hosted just over one hundred campers—two thousand youngsters had been served. At times, the campgrounds felt like it was bursting at its seams, so the county made another land purchase from the Places, this one adding an important eight hundred feet of Lake Ontario shore.

As the 1950s gave way to the '60s, despite some lean financial times, support for Camp Hollis continued. Along with the County of Oswego and charitable organizations like Oswego and Fulton's Community Chest, there were smaller, but equally meaningful, contributions. The Women's Club of the Fulton Chamber of Commerce held a bake sale and raised $110.65 for the camp. Also continuing to hold up its end of the bargain was the State of New York's Youth Commission. Its 50 percent reimbursement of camp expenses was now being promoted nationally, referring to Camp Hollis as a "model of its success."

Judge Sullivan, now in his sixties, began cutting back his day-to-day involvement with the camp. Sullivan's son, Pat, who'd been Hollis's camp director in 1954 and '55, joined the county's Recreation Committee, which had assumed many of the judge's responsibilities. Among the duties the younger Sullivan inherited from his father was the hiring of a good camp director. One of Pat's hires was Ed Garno, who would one day be Oswego's superintendent of schools. But in the summer of 1962, Ed's main concern was Camp Hollis. He reflected on that in 1996, when the camp celebrated its fifty-year anniversary:

Pat Sullivan was our boss and he was deeply involved and a wonderful man to work with. His affection for the campers and camp lore was matched by his large stature, roaring laugh and genuine concern for people, young and old alike. The children benefitted from the dedicated and highly qualified teachers and college graduates who made up our staff. After a first day orientation, the campers enjoyed programs including health practices, quality nutrition, arts & crafts, story hours, athletics, field trips, cookouts on the beach and a variety of competitions. Only later did I understand that the personal experiences at Camp Hollis were far more valuable and meaningful than any salary.

Harvey Smith followed Ed Garno, serving as camp director in 1963 and '64. Harvey recognized how much the campers enjoyed Hollis's campfire singalongs, so he compiled an official songbook. Counselors could choose among thirty-seven tunes, which read like a who's who of summer camp songs. There were '60s folk classics like "This Land Is Your Land," spirituals like "He's Got the Whole World in His Hands," classics like "Shine on Harvest Moon" and a few Lewis's Bluff originals like "Hollis Will Shine" and "The Hollis Spirit."

By the end of the 1960s, Oswego County's Recreation Commission had created a year-round position that would assume responsibility for parks and recreation programs, including Camp Hollis. Parks and Recreation directors like Alan Foster made sure that the camp operated according to New York State Health Codes and its staff provided quality youth activities. Some of those who were responsible for the children had long tenures at the camp, including Pat Cloonan (1968–74). After spending a summer as a Hollis camper and then several years at a Boy Scout camp, Pat started working at Camp Hollis while in college:

I was a counselor from 1968 until '72 and then became the site director from 1973 to '74. There were several counselors who worked the same summers I did, and we had a close staff. After the kids were in bed, anyone who wasn't on duty would go down to the bluff to sit together and talk. If the weather wasn't great, we'd congregate in the kitchen and eat. The rule was we could eat anything that wasn't on the menu for the next day. Sometimes, in between sessions, we would go to an amusement park together or to Camp Director Herb Hammond's [1970–71] camp in New Hampshire.

Cloonan led Arts & Crafts, recalling that "we painted a lot of rocks and because I had learned how to do boondoggle at the Scout camp, we did that, too. I didn't have much of a budget, but I bought some supplies at

Howard's Office Supplies and Aero Supply in Oswego." Pat entertained at campfires with the song "Chester," which came in handy during his long teaching career. "I taught the song and hand motions to all my classes. I still substitute teach at that school and I'm still teaching the song."

Hollis's reputation as a summer camp that welcomed all children grew, as did the waiting list for those anxious to attend. To address this, in 1974 the camp made a significant change to its program session, trimming a child's stay to one week—actually, six days.* Although the move doubled the number of children accepted to attend, the waiting list persisted. The problem, Hollis supervisors came to see, wasn't having sufficient space for daytime activities. What the camp lacked was enough room in its dormitories for additional beds. One year later, the county addressed that need.

Steve McDonough (Oswego City-County Youth Bureau Director, 1973–80), was involved with the plan to boost Hollis's camper numbers. Steve became the first director of its newly formed Youth Bureau and later inherited oversight of Camp Hollis after the county dissolved its Recreation Commission.† A major Hollis project underway at this time was the county's acquisition of another twenty acres of property on Lewis's Bluff, again doubling the size of the campgrounds. Then, in 1975, Steve found himself overseeing the county's purchase of three sleepaway cabins. They were "do it yourself" log cabins from Sears & Roebuck, and McDonough had a sizable challenge getting them habitable:

> *Work began on the cabins at the first thaw of 1975, courtesy of the County Highway Department and the Buildings & Grounds Department. No sooner had we gotten the buildings framed up than we were visited by the County Health Department, who told us we'd be required to expand our septic system in order to get an operating certificate. Right on their heels came the Fire Marshal, who told us we couldn't open if we didn't put "panic bar" hardware on the doors. Yes, it was a regular inspectors' convention out there for a while. We finally finished the cabins though; outfitted, dedicated and opened in time for the season. That summer, we took twice as many kids.*

---

* Initially, the shorter session started Monday morning and ended Saturday morning. By the 1990s, the start and end days were Sunday night through Friday afternoon.

† In 1974, the county and the city of Oswego combined their Youth Bureaus, creating the Oswego City-County Youth Bureau.

In 1975, two days before Christmas, Judge Sullivan passed away. Camp Hollis, boarded up for the season and hibernating under a blanket of snow, remained silent. But all over Oswego County, hundreds of former counselors hired by the judge and thousands of children who got their chance at summer camp fun offered a special holiday prayer for the man who'd made it all possible.

As Judge Sullivan would have hoped, Oswego County continued to work on welcoming all children to Camp Hollis. In 1977 and 1980, four buildings were erected on the grounds. They were designed as twin cabins, with each side sleeping eight or nine campers and a pair of counselors, again increasing enrollment. Shortly after, the county committed to serving one hundred children per week, and plans were made to build a final set of double cabins. That did not happen until 1994, and in the meantime, two army-style canvas tents were erected. Living in them was sometimes too close to nature, especially when Lake Ontario stirred up wind and rainstorms. Counselors were rotated in and out of tent duty to "share the wealth."

By the 1980s, Camp Hollis had established itself as a reliable youth program with talented staff that provided a variety of recreational activities on acres of lakefront property. Add in three meals and a snack and who could want for more? Everything seemed perfect until an old problem resurfaced. It had to do with the camp's main building again, but this time moving it wouldn't help.

Camp officials and the county had been aware of the building's dwindling life expectancy as early as 1962. That August, County Legislators passed a resolution to hire an architect who would develop options for an expansion of Camp Hollis buildings. The Legislators agreed that the main building needed attention, but the county had dozens of facilities to operate and plans to replace the Hollis structure were shelved. Two decades later, county officials knew that they could wait no longer.

By 1982, the building, constructed almost entirely of wood and more than fifty years old, was deteriorating at an alarming rate. It was Judy McManus (1974, 1981–86), the Oswego City-County Youth Bureau's year-round supervisor of Camp Hollis, who had to operate camp from the building. "It was falling apart," Judy recalled. "The foundations were shifting, the walls were leaning at a noticeable slant and the wood building was judged a fire hazard."

Indeed, the threat of fire was significant. Fire department inspectors estimated that an undetected flare-up would engulf the main building in minutes. Once this risk was made clear, counselors were required to add an additional task to their busy schedule: fire watch. Assigned two-hour shifts between midnight and 6:00 a.m., staff walked the perimeter of the main building while shining a flashlight under the structure, looking for signs of fire. Aside from further tiring the already-exhausted counselors, fire watch meant having to face the dead-of-night darkness alone, a challenge for even the bravest staff members.

When Patricia Mears (Oswego City-County Youth Bureau Director, 1980–87) was appointed, she was well aware of the Hollis building's problems. Patti had been a Camp Hollis lifeguard/counselor in the 1970s and knew that the structure was in desperate need of attention. There was talk of closing the camp due to the huge expense of addressing the building's problems. To tackle this dilemma and determine the future of Camp Hollis, Patti created a committee of twenty-three county officials and community leaders. As she recalled:

> There were a range of opinions of what should happen to the camp. One suggestion was to level the building and turn the facility into a day program. Another idea was to scrap the camp entirely and find another use for the property. Some wanted to keep it a residential camp but thought the old building should be replaced with a pole barn, which didn't make sense for a camp that needed a full kitchen, administrative offices and a nurse's station. Fortunately, there were some on the committee who went to bat for the camp, like Director of Personnel Carolyn Rush; Art Ospelt, County Highway Superintendent; and Legislator Hollis Iselin.

Iselin represented the town of Schroeppel, and he had a soft spot in his heart for the camp. Not just because he was named after Dr. LeRoy Hollis, who attended the Legislator's birth, but also because Iselin loved children. When some elected officials suggested cutting the county's losses and shutting the camp down, he wouldn't hear of it:

> I wanted a new building and new cabins. I didn't want children sleeping where cooking and recreation were. There was opposition on the floor from legislators who figured it wouldn't work. But I had dreams for the future. I thought about what it would look like when the county was growing with more children. Should we wait for a crisis, or think and plan ahead?

Iselin made a convincing argument, and in August 1982, County Legislators voted to set aside $80,000 for the new structure. Over the winter

Oswego County Legislator Hollis Iselin, from the town of Schroeppel, was a longtime supporter of Camp Hollis and children's programs. *Courtesy of the Camp Hollis Archives.*

months, they solicited bids for the building's construction, with blueprints showing a larger dining hall/group recreational area, industrial-sized kitchen, administrative and nursing offices and rooms where camp senior staff would reside during the summer. All bids, of course, needed to meet current fire codes but also were to include cost estimates for weatherproofing and insulation. Was the county intending to make the facility usable year-round? A closer inspection of the blueprints answered that question. The plans did not include heat for the building.

Legislators were disappointed to find that the lowest bid, from R.W. Clark Contracting, of Camillus, came in $53,119 above the $80,000 approved for the project. More discussion within legislative chambers took place, and in February 1983, that additional amount was added. The Youth Bureau, excited to be operating camp out of a "healthier" building, announced step one of the process. That month, in an attempt to get a jump on the demolition and construction work, county workers attempted to move one of the old building's dormitory wings.

"It was to become the camp's Arts & Crafts building," Judy McManus remembered. "Unfortunately, it had been a rainy season and the tractors that were going to pull the dorm a few hundred feet got stuck in the mud. The move happened, but only after things dried out."

The wet spring also pushed back the date for the start of new construction into April, which had a lot of children nervous that there might not be a Camp Hollis that summer. A May *Palladium-Times* article put their worries to rest, reporting the county's intention to operate the camp. And it did, albeit one week late, cutting the 1983 season from eight weeks to seven. "My staff's pre-camp training included a lot of cleaning and getting the new building ready," McManus explained. "When we learned that the kitchen wouldn't be finished in time to serve our first meals, we hauled food back and forth from St Paul's Parish Hall in Oswego."

Over the years, Oswego County has made good on the other improvements suggested by Patti Mears's "Future of Camp Hollis" committee. In 1989, the county's Buildings & Grounds Department erected a maintenance shed to store lawn mowers, work tools and, through a donation from Alcan (today known as Novelis), a motorized cart for hauling garbage and moving

On a cold, wet spring day in 1983, a section of Hollis's original main building was moved to create the camp's Arts & Crafts center. *Courtesy of the Camp Hollis Archives.*

70

supplies. The following year, B&G added an additional meeting area on the campgrounds: an open-air pavilion situated perfectly for groups to enjoy a front-row seat at the lake.

Physical upgrades to Camp Hollis have sometimes been made by its summer staff. Back in the 1950s, counselors' pre-camp training often included "painting everything inside and outside the camp 'Judge Sullivan green,'" staff person Joanie Koster Mayhew (1953–55) remembered. Some years, staff chose a location on the campgrounds for a makeover. A 1990s staff created "Nature's Nook," a quiet area where small groups could gather under shade trees. In 1993, counselor Brent Jones (1992–96) showed up for his summer job with a gift from his father, Charles Jones:

> *Dad made a totem pole from a felled tree, using a chainsaw and wood chisels to carve the totem's spirit animals from the New York Five Nations Indian tribes: bear, wolf, turtle, deer, beaver, and hawk. He made the hawk wings in his woodshop. I thought the pole would be a good way for campers to learn about the Native American history in our area.*

The camp found a perfect location for Brent's totem pole when a new building was added to the growing campgrounds. But this one wouldn't be built by county workers or a construction company; in fact, it wouldn't even be built on Lewis's Bluff. Kathy Fenlon (Oswego City-County Youth Bureau Director, 1987–2013) remembered the unique circumstances that gave Camp Hollis its latest building:

> *It was an Arts & Crafts building constructed by BOCES Technical Career class. The county provided funds for the materials and supplies, and the BOCES Building Trades Program's teacher and students built a 24x48-foot building in the style of a modular home. On a bright and sunny June 1995 day, the building was transported, in two pieces, from the BOCES campus to Camp Hollis. Within the space of an hour, it was rolled off the trailers and onto the waiting foundation—it fit like a glove! Amazing!*

One improvement to the Camp Hollis property drew loud cheers from longtime staff and returning campers. In 1997, Hollis joined its town of Oswego neighbors in welcoming city water lines to the area. After decades of trying to drink a glass of sulfur-smelling well water (let alone brushing their teeth with it), everyone was happy to turn on a faucet and not have to hold their nose.

A new Arts & Crafts building was constructed offsite at Oswego County BOCES and delivered to the camp in two sections. *Courtesy of the Camp Hollis Archives.*

In 1999, Camp Hollis received buildings and grounds support from Leadership Oswego County (LOC). Administered by SUNY Oswego's Office of Business and Community Relations, LOC provides training for those interested in civic matters. Each class is challenged to put their knowledge to work with a project they design and implement. That year's future leaders showed up at Hollis with shovels, lumber and rope, ready to create a new trail that would guide campers down a steep hill to a stream. Every child who has since stepped into that stream and lifted a rock to discover tadpoles, crayfish or water spiders has LOC to thank.

With new buildings and points of interest on the campgrounds to enjoy, some children who'd outgrown the camper role didn't want the fun to end. Camp administrators acknowledged the value of continuing to welcome all ages by creating two programs: a thirteen- and fourteen-year-old week, which replaced the traditional camp schedule with activities that catered to young teens—competitive swimming, mural painting, staging a play—and a counselor-in-training program for fifteen- and sixteen-year-olds. Finally, those who loved Camp Hollis since their first year as a camper wouldn't have to skip a single year on the path to becoming a counselor.

The new millennium welcomed more improvements. In 2006, the main building "grew" by thirty-six feet. It came in the form of a classroom built for BOCES's Deaf Education Summer School, which had been taking place elsewhere on the campgrounds. With generous donations from groups like the John Ben Snow Foundation and the Fulton and Oswego Lions Clubs, the additional indoor space made rainy days a little more tolerable. In sunnier

Great Moments in the History of the World

weather, camp enjoyed a gift from Entergy, owner of an Oswego nuclear power plant. It was a sturdy ramp that stretched from camp property to the rocky beach, eliminating harmful foot traffic on the eroding bluff.

Year after year, Oswego County and Camp Hollis leaders continued to build on Dr. Hollis's and Judge Sullivan's dream. As generations of children enjoyed camp, stories spread of their fun at Lewis's Bluff. While talk was generally positive, the public's awareness of the camp was sometimes hindered by a misconception that persisted. For its first decade and a half, Lewis's Bluff was home to a health camp working to prevent the spread of tuberculosis. When it was reopened by a Children's Court judge, it seemed like the camp only served orphans or children in trouble. Was Camp Hollis really a place where *all* boys and girls were welcome?

As early as 1950, county and Hollis leaders tried to dispel the idea that it only served certain children. The camp's first director, H.H. Stevens, stated in a letter to parents that "[Camp Hollis] is not a health camp, nor a camp for delinquents or underprivileged children. It's a camp for well-behaved girls and boys of Oswego County."

It would take many years (and in some ways the misunderstanding continues) for Hollis to be seen as a haven for all children who could benefit from a summer camp experience. In order for that fact to be broadly accepted, its staff would spend summer after summer providing boys and girls with one jam-packed day of fun after another.

FROM SUNUP TO SUNDOWN

No matter if they attended Dr. Hollis's Health Camp in the 1930s, Judge Sullivan's camp in the 1960s or the new millennium's version, what children experience at Lewis's Bluff has remained remarkably similar. Ask anyone who's ever spent a summer at Camp Hollis and you'll hear the same story: It's a long day and it starts early—with a big splash.

Known as POLAR BEAR SWIM, it's been the first activity of every Camp Hollis morning since children and their counselors have gathered at Lewis's Bluff. And why shouldn't it be? When a Great Lake is your nearest neighbor, you might as well take full advantage.

There's no written record of who first decided to begin the day with a dip. I imagine it was modeled after those brave souls who take a cold-water plunge to ceremonially start the New Year. One evening, early in Camp Hollis history, a counselor, perhaps trying to impress the rest of the staff, challenged campers with this campfire announcement: "I'm getting up before breakfast to go for a swim. Who wants to join me?" "I do!" a majority of campers exclaimed, along with a couple counselors, who were pretty sure the whole thing was a joke.

It might have sounded like fun huddled around that fire, but as counselor Tom Roshau (1985–87) recalled, "Polar Bear is a terrific idea at bedtime, but morning arrives way too early." Still, a few of the hardier children—the ones who didn't want to waste a minute of their Camp Hollis day—accepted that counselor's dare, and the Polar Bear Swim was created. Once established, the challenge was expanded: participate every morning and you're in the

"I think the Polar Bear Club pushed the envelope just a little too far this morning."

Polar Bear Club. Over the years, that would earn campers a felt badge in the shape of a polar bear's head, an official-looking card modeled after Red Cross swimming certificates or a colorful award signed by Hollis's waterfront director. They were tangible proof of a camper's bravery and ended up tacked to bedroom walls for years.

If a dormitory or cabin had an enthusiastic counselor, the whole group could end up at Polar Bear Swim. But staff members willing to forgo a half hour of sleep were rare, so they taught campers to make a construction paper sign with "Yes" written on one side and "No" on the other. The signs hung by camper beds, and when a lifeguard tapped on the door and tiptoed in to wake Polar Bears, the sign indicated each camper's decision. Many a child went to bed with a confident "Yes" on display but flipped it over before daybreak. Beds can be so warm and the morning air so cold.

But not as cold as Lake Ontario in early morning, especially after a thunderstorm churns up its waters and frigid temperatures from the bottom of the lake rise to the surface. Even after Polar Bear Swim started taking place in the pool, cool evenings rapidly lowered its temperature. John Baumann (1982–86) remembered marching his boys down to Lake Ontario. "The campers would jump in and splash around," John said. "It also helped me, not usually a morning person, to wake up."

⟳⟳⟳

John played a role in another early morning activity, this one involving the whole campgrounds as well as Hollis's neighbors. It's the MORNING WAKEUP CALL. "Sometimes I got up early," John admitted, "and woke each cabin by playing reveille, pointing my trombone in through cabin windows." Depending on the year, other instruments spread that rousing wakeup song throughout the sleepy camp. Counselors had fun putting their high school band skills to good use. Trumpets, French horns, tubas and, during one particularly irritating summer, a set of drums crushed any hope for a few extra minutes of shuteye.

Each day begins with campers and staff circling the flagpole to watch the United States and Oswego County flags being raised. *Courtesy of the Camp Hollis Archives.*

Wide awake or not, five minutes before breakfast, the entire camp shows up for FLAG RAISING. Once gathered around the flagpole, the chatter of campers retelling stories of last night's activity quiets. Hats come off and hands rest over hearts as all eyes watch the American flag, followed by the Camp Hollis or Oswego County flag, slowly rise like the sun. Sometimes, a lucky camper is chosen to clip the flag to the guide rope; another child gives the rope rhythmic tugs until the flag takes its place at the top of the pole. One hundred or more voices pledge allegiance, and on some particularly beautiful mornings, the director urges young and old alike to turn toward the lake and reflect on the gift of another day at Camp Hollis.

Many former counselors and campers will tell you that no meal has ever tasted better than a Camp Hollis BREAKFAST. There's something about waking up surrounded by nature, especially after a chilly Polar Bear dip, that makes the first bite of food so satisfying. Even for those who slept in, once the smell of pancakes grilling or cinnamon oatmeal bubbling drifts to their beds…well, there's nothing like it.

"The food was wonderful and plentiful," remembered William Dickerson, who grew up in an Oswego orphanage. "Like the camp itself, it fed my deeply felt hunger for a better life." According to Craig Fisher, it didn't matter what was on the Camp Hollis breakfast menu. "They had those little boxes of different kinds of cereal and I could choose whatever one I wanted—and I could have seconds!"

The person responsible for all those memorable meals, the kitchen manager, puts in long hours, and when it comes to breakfast, she and her helpers are at work before the Polar Bears take their dip. One person who made many of those meals was Jean Crouch, who ran the Camp Hollis kitchen from 1973 through 1980. Jean was a single mother raising five children, and as she mentioned in her recollections of the camp, "It wasn't just a summer job—it was a family affair!" Some years, like 1976, nearly all the Crouch children worked alongside their mother and were affectionately known as the "Crouch Kitchen." "One summer, we pitched tents in the woods so we could live right at camp," Jean remembered.

Even when the Crouches commuted from home each morning, they spent more time at camp than their own house. "My youngest child, Jeanette, was camper-aged when I first started," Jean explained. "I'd drive into camp with her asleep in the car and let her sleep while I got breakfast started. When she woke up, she'd come in and start helping in the kitchen."

In addition to three meals a day, Jean made sure that campers had an evening snack and plenty of cold beverages throughout the day. In between cooking big vats of spaghetti or grilling a couple dozen whole chickens, she also had to keep supply shelves stocked. When ordering food, Jean made sure she kept the most popular items on hand, including peanut butter; she estimated going through about 150 pounds of the sandwich spread per summer. Of course, it takes more than sandwiches to run a camp—a lot more. Youth Bureau director Steve McDonough knew that the camp was in good hands, food-wise, when he first met Jean:

> *Before working for the Youth Bureau, I served six years in the National Guard, most of it as a cook. So I was aware of what it takes to prepare, serve and clean up meals for large groups. I understood the enormity of what Jean had to do and from the first time I met her, I knew she could do it. Sure enough, year after year, the Camp Hollis kitchen went off without a single hitch.*

Both children and staff loved the special camp meals, like apple fritters for breakfast, that kitchen manager Jean Crouch made from scratch. *Courtesy of the Camp Hollis Archives.*

It wasn't just campers gobbling up Jean's yummy breakfasts; counselors loved it when she whipped up their morning favorite: apple fritters. "I used to make plenty extra because staff would come into the kitchen for leftovers," Jean said. "Sometimes I'd get 10 or 12 counselors hanging out in the kitchen, and I'd have to chase them out so I could get some work done. Secretly, I really enjoyed feeding them."

Jean was also an artist, and whenever she could find a few minutes, she painted camp scenes on beach rocks. She also sketched the fence along the bluff and the old pump house, which for years was featured on Camp Hollis T-shirts.

Following Jean's tenure in the kitchen was Lois Terminella, who holds the record for the most years anyone has worked at Camp Hollis: forty and counting. Lois was hired after working a few years in a nursing home kitchen, and she learned a lot in her first Hollis summers, including the fact that she enjoyed food service. Shortly after she started running the Hollis kitchen, Lois was hired by SUNY Oswego's Auxiliary Services, and that school year dining hall job allowed her to continue as Camp Hollis's kitchen manager summer after summer.

One reason Lois keeps coming back year after year is that she enjoys creating popular meals, including her pancakes—especially when she drops chocolate chips into the batter—and she knows kids always ask for seconds and thirds of her goulash. Everyone—campers *and* counselors—looks forward to her weekly cookout, no matter what's on the grill. Lois explained how she decides which meals get a big thumbs up:

> *I make it a practice to always check on the kids to see that they're eating and enjoying the meal. I train my staff to take over at the stove or the meal prep so I can spend time in the dining hall. It makes me feel good, knowing that kids enjoy what I plan and cook. I know that to some campers mealtime is a real treat.*

Lois takes note of her popular dishes and remembers them when it comes time to place a food order. Nutritional standards have changed over the years and she works with that information while planning meals. Food orders always include plenty of milk; as in the founding days of Camp Hollis, today's campers still receive glassfuls at each meal and evening snack. Lois places her milk order with the same company that she's used since starting her Hollis job. Each week she calls Hudson's Dairy, a family-owned business in Fulton, to order milk—156 gallons of it. "Sometimes," Lois said, "I run out and have to make a quick trip to a local store."

Even when the camp runs smoothly, it's a delicate balance of knowing how much to keep on hand and when the kitchen will need more. Planning gets tougher if there's an unexpected interruption in the schedule, like what happened back in the 1990s, when a major storm shut down Lois's kitchen with a three-day power outage:

My food vendors had just delivered the week's supply of freezer and cooler foods and there I was with no electricity. I had to find some place to store the food—and fast. I called the owner of Rudy's Lakeside Drive-in, Carol Livesey, who graciously said yes. I loaded everything in a vehicle and Rudy's kept it until camp's power was restored. Thanks to Carol, I didn't lose a single item of perishable food.

Managing camp's food supply and offering children their favorite meals are big parts of Lois's job, but they aren't the main reason she comes back every year. It's because of her staff. Most of the Hollis kitchen helpers are young, as young as sixteen, and it's a first job for most of them. Lois knows that the kitchen isn't why most teens want to work at Hollis, but she tries to instill pride in her staff and expects them to develop a strong work ethic. "I tell my staff I can't do it without them," Lois said. "Some struggle and they worry they'll lose their job. But I tell them that I'll work with them and that by the end of the summer, they'll feel good about what we've accomplished."

Evidence of Lois's achievements in her four decades of helping young people succeed can be seen at the camp's cookout area, where her workers have prepped, served and cleaned up countless picnic meals. On a sign nailed to a post are these words engraved in wood: "2006. Dedicated to Lois Terminella."

━∿∿∿━

Though no one's favorite activity, the next event on Camp Hollis's schedule, MORNING CLEANUP, is certainly necessary. Imagine living with 150 people and having no rules for cleanliness or order. To keep things tidy at Hollis, cleanup procedures were originally modeled after an organization known for its high standards: the U.S. Army. "The counselors taught us to make our beds military style," William Dickerson said, "with sheets and blankets neatly folded into corners at the bottom, then everything tucked in.[Parents were impressed when their children came home from camp knowing how to make a bed with "hospital corners."] Then the counselors would do an inspection, flipping a quarter onto the bed. If it didn't bounce, they tore the bed apart and made us do it again."

Counselors don't stop with insisting on perfect beds. Campers are also assigned to sweep floors (to earn a few extra points at inspection, some even swab the deck), neatly fold clothes, pick up litter around the dorms or cabins and, least desirable of all, scrub toilets. Before the fun of the day can begin, living spaces are scrutinized by an inspector. That job has been handled by different staff members. Cindy Czerow Nacey remembered how Camp Director Bob Bellinger "would come in to inspect the boys' and the girls' dormitories. Mr. B announced the winner each day and that side got to raise a banner in their dorm."

There have been other ways to determine who has the cleanest living space. Some inspectors keep score, with a cabin earning anywhere from ten points for a super-clean morning to zero for a disaster. The numbers are totaled up on the last day of camp, and the hardworking winners get to slip a "Cleanest Cabin" certificate in their suitcases. A few counselors go the extra mile to claim the prize, teaching campers how to stand at attention and salute when the inspector arrives or sending campers out to pick wildflowers so they can greet the inspector with a colorful bouquet. Some groups break out in the inspector's favorite song.

While counselors and campers are busy thinking how to please the inspector, those rating living spaces also get creative. Perhaps the best example of inventive inspecting came from Doug Roshau (1983–88). More than thirty years later, Doug—along with hundreds of other staff and campers—still recalls a time when the "Ninja Inspector" ruled Camp Hollis:

> *Just prior to my tenure at camp, inspections were carried out by Assistant Director Forrest LaBarre [1981–83, '96], who conducted them disguised as his "twin brother," dressed in an old army uniform and wielding a no-nonsense military mindset. When it became my job to take over inspections, the Ninja Inspector was born, complete with a makeshift Karate Kid ensemble, including a white mask, headband, flip flops and broom handle walking staff.*
>
> *The Ninja Inspector never uttered a word during his appearances, and since a different person played the role each day—directors, counselors, nurses, kitchen staff and even a young camper (great job, Wendy!)—campers and staff never knew his true identity. The Ninja Inspector was always escorted by a staff person, not only speaking as "the voice of Ninja," but, more importantly, buffering the Ninja from his many unruly fans.*
>
> *The Ninja's rounds occurred each afternoon during Free Swim, when the entire camp was tucked safely behind by the closed gate of the pool. For the most part, Ninja inspections were "fair and just," often involving the Ninja's personal credos in life, such as: "A full wastebasket…is an empty wastebasket!" These words would be announced in booming voice by the*

Escort just prior to the Ninja dumping the cabin's full wastebasket on the front lawn. On more than one occasion (if the Ninja was exceptionally appalled at a cabin's lack of cleanliness), mattresses, sleeping bags and pillows would be tossed out the front door or on the cabin's roof, all to the enjoyment of the onlooking crowd.

Campers loved to hate the Ninja. As he moved from cabin to cabin, the energy level of his audience would rise exponentially. It was not uncommon, even on the hottest days, to see the pool completely empty of swimmers; instead, everyone lined along the pool fence, rattling the gate and shouting insults at the stoic figure: "We hate you, Ninja!" "You stink, Ninja!"

Over the years, the Ninja's legend grew as stories were passed from campers to siblings, cousins and friends. Children who'd never attended Camp Hollis would arrive, announcing to staff, "That Ninja better not touch my stuff if he knows what's good for him." Instead of questions about camp activities being offered that week, countless kids were consumed by the Ninja and his shenanigans, wanting to know if he was indeed real and when they might see him.

Without a doubt, the Ninja Inspector's most infamous moment came during the summer of 1987, when counselors Joe Eldred, Tom Roshau and I devised a social experiment involving the Ninja. Instead of him conducting afternoon inspections that week, the camp was set upon by the "Night Ninja," an imposing figure resembling a hooded medieval executioner. A dark brown robe, stomping boots, looming hood and barely discernable eye holes kept anyone from knowing that I was the person behind this new character.

Whereas the Ninja was always "fair and just," the Night Ninja followed no such protocol. He stormed from cabin to cabin, striding alone (no escort would dare join him) and indiscriminately scattering blankets and sleeping bags in his wake—even those that had been tidy and neat! No camper or counselor was immune from the Night Ninja's wrath, raising his plastic battle axe in defiance at those foolish enough to question his judgment.

The campers in the pool area that first afternoon stared in silence at the Night Ninja. They'd heard Ninja stories and were ready with their typical responses. But the appearance of the Night Ninja? No one had warned them about this! That first afternoon was quick and messy, with the Night Ninja exiting the scene before camp had a chance to realize what had befallen it.

Needless to say, there was quite a buzz at dinner that evening, with much speculation about the Night Ninja's origin. I informed the campers at my table that I had once heard tales of him but had never actually witnessed

Cabin Inspector: Must be capable of enduring the wrath of countless children.

My, how promising!!

him until today. The stage was now set for the Great Camp Hollis Social Experiment.

The very next afternoon, the Night Ninja arrived again on cue. This time, however, the campers were ready for him, hurling insults as he began trashing the first cabin. Unbeknownst to the campers and other staff, Joe and Tom were hidden in Cabin 4, with Tom dressed as the original Ninja and Joe as his escort. No sooner had the Night Ninja entered Cabin 4, when suddenly he came stumbling backwards through the door, landing on the lawn in a tangled heap. Standing in the doorway of Cabin 4, in all his glory, was the Ninja. At his side, the escort decreed in a booming voice, "All hail the true Ninja Inspector!"

Immediately the pool area erupted in raucous cheers. Elation turned to shock, however, as they realized the Night Ninja was unwilling to relinquish his crown quite so easily. Cabin 4's front lawn was about to become the arena where this feud would be settled.

As previously choreographed, the two Ninjas battled, feeding off the campers' cheers and jeers. The confrontation ended with the original Ninja using his wooden staff to knock the battle axe from the Night Ninja's grip, knocking him to the ground. Defeated, the Night Ninja rose to his knees while the Ninja grabbed the dark hood, ready to pull it off and reveal the Night Ninja's true identity.

According to plan, the Night Ninja (me) was wearing a paper bag underneath my hood. When the original Ninja pulled off my hood, I was to have a tight hold on the bag, keeping my identity hidden while I made my escape. As the Ninja turned toward the campers and sought their decision, I grabbed desperately for the bag, knowing I only had seconds before the hood would be removed. In a scene straight from the Roman Coliseum, I heard the campers chanting their ascent: "Do it! Do it! Do it!" As the hood was lifted, I found myself unable to grip the bag. Suddenly, with both hood and paper bag removed, I felt sunlight hit my face.

In a final attempt to conceal my identity, I buried my face in my hands, spun away from the crowd and awkwardly crawled my way into the woods, never to return. In the distance, I heard cheers as the Ninja finished his rounds. Even though he was still intent on punishing untidy cabins, the *audience cried out in absolute agreement: "We love you, Ninja!" "You're the best, Ninja!"*

The Great Social Experiment had been a success. The campers' opinion of the Ninja Inspector had forever changed…at least for a few days!

Even after Doug moved on from Hollis, the legend of his Ninja Inspector continued, traveling far beyond the camp. Almost three decades later, Doug's nephew, Marshall Roshau (2015–16), couldn't wait to tell his uncle that he'd bumped into a former camper who just happened to be at camp the very afternoon of the Ninja Battle. Marshall listened as the former camper became lost again in the excitement and memories of that faraway time and place. "It was incredible," Marshall told his Uncle Doug. "This guy could still see everything, just as though it happened yesterday. He could still describe the Ninja Battle word for word!"

———

Certainly, children need hearty meals and clean living quarters at camp, but it's the DAILY ACTIVITIES—the fun—that kids look forward to. Over the years, the activities Hollis offers have changed, sometimes due to a shift in recreational philosophies or fads. (Anybody remember Cooperative Games?) Some new ideas work for a few years; others are forgotten by autumn. There are, however, activities that remain just as popular today as when they first were enjoyed. Leading that popularity contest is the activity many campers consider their favorite.

From 1928's Health Camp until Hollis built its first pool in 1969, SWIMMING took place in Lake Ontario. Some summers, the daily schedule called for six hours of water fun a day. That, of course, depended on the weather. Although it's the smallest of the five Great Lakes, that doesn't mean Ontario is the safest. On stormy days, taking a dip is next to impossible, and not just for fear of getting struck by lightning. A lake storm's crashing waves easily picked up the cement-filled buckets holding Hollis's buoy lines in place, tossing them ashore. After the waters calmed, lifeguards dragged the buckets back out and dropped them in place. Campers were back in the water, where handfuls of fresh seaweed were used in a sloppy version of dodgeball. As counselor Sarah Gould Hill (1976–78) remembered, "Those water games were followed by hours of brushing green gook out of my campers' long hair."

Despite the changeable weather, campers made plenty of swimming memories at Hollis. Judge Sullivan's son Mike, who attended Red Cross Aquatic School at the urging of his dad, noted that "we taught a lot of kids how to swim who had never been near water." Before anyone jumped in, though, campers got divided into ability levels, with areas roped off for Beginners, Intermediates and Swimmers. Just taking the test was a challenge, as former camper Don Todd remembered:

> *I was a Beginner my first year at Hollis and we were told to just walk out in the water to start. There were waves coming in that day and I felt myself going up and down with them. I started to move back to shore, but I got caught by an undertow and couldn't get my head above water. I knew that counselors were close by, so I raised my hand and felt the sun hitting it. Then I felt myself get pulled up and out, having only swallowed a little lake water.*

From that tough introduction to Camp Hollis aquatics, Don and other campers worked hard to pass the swim test; nobody wanted to be stuck in the Beginners section day after day. Some worked their whole session or even a second year at camp before they made it to Intermediates or Swimmer level. Doing so was such an important accomplishment that local newspapers regularly listed the names of Hollis campers who'd achieved the goal. Along with seeing their name in print, campers also earned Arts & Crafts–designed certificates, patches or ribbons.

Keeping track of Swimmers and non-Swimmers required an organized lakefront. A counselor handy with hammer and nails put together the first Camp Hollis Buddy Board, a rectangular piece of plywood color-coded for swim levels and adorned with hooks. After their swim test, boys and girls anxious to dive in had to first hang their nametag next to a friend of a similar

Children braved the sometimes choppy Lake Ontario waters to pass their swimming test. *Courtesy of the Camp Hollis Archives.*

swim level—their buddy. What pride campers felt when they could move their tag to the next level, seeing it catch the sun's rays.

This year I'm earning that swim tag!

Those tags stayed in place (unless a storm swept them away) until the last day of camp, when children could slip them from the Buddy Board into their pocket. Bill Syrell kept his tag from his years as a camper in the 1970s. Forty year later, after he and I had talked about his Camp Hollis memories, Bill dug through his collection of boyhood keepsakes, looking for his swim tag. "Just finding it after all this time seems to me a minor miracle. It's one of my Camp Hollis treasures."

Memories of Lake Ontario aren't all as delightful as earning a swimmer's tag; one, in particular, is downright nauseating. During a certain era of Camp Hollis—the 1950s through the '60s—children had to share their swimming area with thousands of unwanted "guests." As camper William Dickerson explained, he needed to be careful to avoid stepping on dead "mooneyes" that washed ashore after storms. "Their rotting bodies exposed bones that hurt to the touch and they smelled to the high heavens," Dickerson remembered.

I recall those mooneyes, too, from my camper days. If someone, or a group of someones—it always seemed to be us boys—had misbehaved, the punishment was to walk the Hollis beach and pick up dead mooneyes. After handling those shriveled and crusted fish, you didn't easily forget them because their smell lingered on your fingers, even after applying a bar of soap. I can still picture those lifeless fish spoiling my picture-perfect memory of the Hollis lakeshore. How did mooneyes land on the camp's beach? And why did they die in such large numbers?

Properly known as alewives or, scientifically, *Alosa pseudoharengus*, it's easy to see how mooneyes got their nickname. A medium-sized silver fish, when alive and swimming they glisten like moonlight on the water. Mooneyes are native to the Atlantic, where they grow to ten or eleven inches; their cousins that call the freshwaters of Lake Ontario home are in the six- to seven-inch range. Was it their smaller size that made so many of them die and wash onto Camp Hollis's shore, stinking up swim time? Well, sort of.

Along with a smaller body, alewives also have a higher salt concentration than Lake Ontario waters. Further stressing their systems is a sensitivity to

"It's our third Mooneye Scavenger Hunt this week. The kids are beginning to suspect something."

temperature fluctuations. As alewives migrate to spawn, they might swim through sections of the lake with varying temperatures, especially after big storms. Over the course of a summer, this might happen two or three times, killing off enough mooneyes to give misbehaving campers plenty of foul-smelling fish to collect.

Today, mooneyes are just a Camp Hollis memory. Beginning in the 1960s, the Pacific salmon, which feeds on alewives, was introduced to Lake Ontario. Around the same time, the water level of the lake began to be artificially lowered and raised to control flooding and protect man-made structures. One of the results of tampering with lake water levels is that small fish like alewives have fewer natural habitats to breed and thrive. With shallow areas of the lake and its tributaries reduced, the mooneye population just about disappeared, but I've never heard a single complaint from anyone at Camp Hollis.

For decades, the only way to cool off during Camp Hollis heat waves was in Lake Ontario. *Courtesy of the Camp Hollis Archives.*

Thankfully, there are plenty of enjoyable experiences to be found on Lake Ontario shores. Camper Christine Fisher explained how she spent time waiting for her turn to swim. "There were rocks on the beach, wonderful smooth stones and pebbles of colors that changed and intensified when they were wet." Along with Christine, thousands of children searched for the prettiest rock and pocketed it as a Camp Hollis swimming memory.

By the late 1960s, New York State health codes for aquatic programs had become more stringent.* Health inspectors took a critical look at how Hollis's buoy lines shifted after storms and determined that method of monitoring swimmers was unsafe. They considered Ontario's destructive waves and powerful undertows to be as severe as an ocean's. In order to keep children swimming in the lake, the codes required major costly upgrades: a portable dock system, lifeguards patrolling from canoes and additional elevated observation chairs on shore. Then someone on the Hollis staff made a suggestion: Why not avoid the lake's changeable nature altogether and build a pool?

In 1969, Hollis's new swimming pool opened to much enthusiasm. Unfortunately, the camp's location and design of the pool had problems.

---

* Today's health inspectors would not have approved of another way Camp Hollis used the lake. In its early years, counselors walked swim-suited campers down to the beach, each carrying a towel and a miniature bar of Ivory Soap. That floatable bar was essential because, once a week, Lake Ontario served as Camp Hollis's bathtub.

By the 1970s, swimming at the camp had shifted to an in-ground pool, eliminating concerns about the lake's frequent ocean-like conditions. *Courtesy of the Camp Hollis Archives.*

Built in a low-lying section of the campgrounds, the in-ground structure quickly flooded with muddy rainwater after downpours, turning it into a murky pond for toads. The pool closed after its first summer, and for the next few seasons, campers anxious to cool off were transported to Oswego State's pool.

Hollis's second attempt at a swimming pool, in 1974, was constructed on higher ground, and this time the camp had a winner. Forty-seven years later, the pool still plays host to hours of aquatic programs. A single buoy line clearly designates its shallow and deep ends. Now when campers are deemed a Swimmer, they're issued a neon pink wrist bracelet, making it easy to see if a non-Swimmer drifts over to the deep end. Just like the swim tags of long ago, wristbands have become a sign of pride for campers. Many keep them on long after returning home, evidence to family and friends that they were a Camp Hollis Swimmer.

Like the change in location of where children swim, ARTS & CRAFTS activities have been enjoyed at various Hollis settings. Children first tried their hand at creative projects under the bluff's shade trees. In the 1950s, a screened-in porch off the girls' dormitory became an open-air art space. When the main building was replaced in the 1980s, one of its dormitory wings was moved a few hundred feet and named the official Arts & Crafts building. It was replaced in 1995 by a BOCES student-built structure. But wherever it's been offered, kids have loved being crafty.

There's one rule every Arts & Crafts director must understand when planning a summer's worth of kid-friendly projects: don't expect a lot of money for supplies. And so, year after year, kids are sent into the woods and along the lakeshore to collect materials: rocks for painting, wildflowers for decorative wall-hangings and leaves for colorful pressings. Some ideas are good for a one-time activity; others have been Hollis mainstays for decades. For example, the Godseye.

Probably what make Godseyes so popular is how easy they are to construct. All it takes is two sticks, found on a woodsy walk, tied together to form a cross. A patient Crafts director then demonstrates how to tie a piece of colorful yarn where the two sticks meet and then weave it from stick to stick. Depending on the sticks' length, completing a Godseye can take a few minutes or multiple craft sessions. But regardless of the time invested, Godseyes are instant works of art, destined for a camper's bedroom wall.

By the time I became a Hollis camper, weaving was still a fun art activity, but our Crafts director was teaching us how to make something more useful: potholders. Metal "looms" helped young fingers stretch brightly colored loops of fabric row by row, and then more loops were snaked over and under those rows. Upon completion, potholders were something we held in our hands with a sense of accomplishment. A half century later, I can still hear our Crafts leader promising, "Your mom will use it every day in her kitchen and hang it there proudly when she's done."

Weaving continues at Hollis today, but the potholder and Godseye have given way to the most popular craft project: boondoggle. With such an unusual name, I consulted with my dictionary to find out exactly what the word means. A boondoggle, Webster's claims, is a "trifling or pointless project." I guess Mr. Webster never spent an afternoon under a playground tree, turning pieces of plastic-coated lacing into works of art.

There are a few dozen ways to make a boondoggle, but the simplest method—the one taught to first-time Hollis campers—requires two pieces of lacing. The pieces are tied together at their middles, creating four strands that head off in different directions, like points on a compass. The north and south strands are turned into two small loops, side by side, and are held in place by forefinger and thumb. The east and west strands are then woven over and under the loops. These steps are repeated for the length of the lacing. Though challenging for even the most nimble fingers, once a camper gets the hang of it, boondoggles provide hours, or sometimes days, of recreation. It comes with a price though. Danielle Barriger Lewis (2008–09) remembered that, as a camper, she loved boondoggling so much she ended up with a handful of blisters.

The colors of a boondoggle's lacing are important. To start, selecting two different shades helps keep track of the different strands. But choosing the right colors also makes for a memorable boondoggle. Stop in at Hollis's Arts & Crafts building on boondoggle day and campers will be quick to share why they chose their colors: "They're my school colors!" "My mom's favorite color is pink!"

Some people have a knack for boondoggling. True devotees to the art—they're known as boondogglers—quickly move beyond the standard two-color box variety. More challenging patterns are the circle weaves, flat braids and spirals. But if you're pattern-challenged, like I am, advancing in the art of boondoggle isn't easy. Many stick with the simple two-strand variety, and once completed, they show up in the most unusual places: on the wrist of your girl or boyfriend or, with a standard metal hook attached, at the end of a jingling set of keys. Others become a bookmark, a door handle for the garden gate or an exotic earring for a night on the town. One way or another, most boondoggles travel home with campers, but now and then, one gets left behind…and with it, a mystery.

No one knows when Hollis's extra-extra-long boondoggle first showed up on the campgrounds. One day, about twenty-five years ago, it appeared, draped over a wall-sized trail map in the main building. It remains there

today, still catching the eye of passersby. Once they realize what they're looking at, people often stop for a closer look. Measuring 104 inches, this boondoggle is woven with an amazing eight strands that somehow worked twelve different colors into rounded, squared and spiral shapes. Somebody must have had a lot of time to spend on "a trifling or pointless project," but Camp Hollis is glad they did!

Some Camp Hollis activities are born out of necessity. Take Nature, for example. During the Health Camp years and the first Camp Hollis seasons, the campgrounds consisted of a single building on the bluff tightly bordered by woods—acres and acres of dense forest with an occasional stream or marshy patch. Other than swimming, outside activities were limited to those woods, which required all those early counselors to be nature directors. Most days, their best activity option was a hike.

Taken on Hollis's only trail, those first hikes were meant to be enjoyable and educational. Camper Christine Fisher remembered that they included "walks along the high cliffs with views of Lake Ontario. The lake seemed to go on forever. We learned useful things like not letting branches slap into the faces of kids behind us, though we sometimes did this intentionally." The hikes were long—counselors knew how useful they were for tiring out campers—but Christine mentioned how they passed the time: "We sang songs like 'I Am a Happy Wanderer.'"

To keep those hikers happy, nature directors carved out a few more trails. But after heading out for a third or fourth woodsy walk of the week, children started complaining. "*Another* hike?" Nature directors learned to expand their activities, and the effort they put into developing interesting outdoor programs can sometimes be life-changing—and not just for children. Just ask former Hollis nature director Jim Hooper (1992–96).

Jim was eighteen and a new high school graduate when he became a counselor at Hollis. He'd worked a few summers at a church camp, where his father was the chaplain, but Jim was looking to expand his experiences. Equally important, his dad's camp was volunteer-driven, and Jim needed money for college. In his first years on the Hollis staff, his potential was evident, and Jim was offered the chance to move up:

> *I was given the opportunity to apply for nature director, though I'd never thought of myself as much of a nature guy. But I gave it some thought and a few weeks later, I said I'd give it a try. I then spent the weeks until camp trying to learn everything I could about the outdoors because I had this idea in my head that, in order to be the nature leader, I had to be able to identify every plant, bug and bird. I talked to a couple of my professors, and they said that identification is a piece of it, but not all of it. They hooked me up with a couple books, and I took a two-week class at [SUNY Oswego's] Rice Creek Field Station.*

Jim turned what he learned into innovative nature activities ranging from flora and fauna study to interactive games and, yes, a few hikes. By the time he returned to college, Jim had discovered that spending a summer in Camp Hollis's natural world had changed his world. He had trouble focusing in his Engineering Science classes, and two years into his declared major, Jim's career goals got murky:

> *My parents were never one to say "Chose a career that can make you a lot of money." They told me I should do something I loved and I knew I loved camp. But could I make a career of it? My mother mentioned that some colleges had a recreation major, and we made site visits to SUNY Brockport and SUNY Cortland. We had a good discussion with Cortland's Dr. Vicki Wilkins, who taught therapeutic recreation classes, and my father asked, "Is he going to get a job in this?" She said, "There's a very good chance. A lot of people need these types of programs."*

It turns out Ms. Wilkins was correct. After graduating college (and working a few more summers at Hollis), Jim was hired by the YMCA's Greenkill Outdoor Environmental Ed Center. The center had an older nature cabin that was being rebuilt while Jim was employed there, and he remembered it when, in 1998, he returned to Camp Hollis through AmeriCorps, a Peace Corps–like program that inspires members to provide a term of service at schools, nonprofits and municipalities. Jim's idea was to rebuild Hollis's Nature Center, complete with displays and activities highlighting the camp's bountiful nature.

While upgrading the camp's nature program, Jim began imagining his future career opportunities. He moved to Ohio and worked seven years as a naturalist in a park environmental education program. In 2005, he was hired as an educator for Cornell University's Cooperative Extension. As part of his responsibilities, today Jim oversees the operation of a children's camp in Canandaigua, New York, enlightening staff on how to use their surroundings to engage children. His ability to see educational and recreational opportunities in a cluster of trees or a babbling brook started at Camp Hollis, when Jim Hooper took a risk by becoming the nature director.

Today, looking at the Camp Hollis grounds, one of its main features is a huge mowed area reaching from the main building to the fence at the bluff. Bordered on one side by a basketball court and a baseball field on the other, the cleared space is big enough for any SPORTS activity a creative counselor can imagine. Having enough room for games has been important to Camp Hollis staff since 1946, when ambitious counselors began clearing trees and removing stumps. As important to children as swimming, crafts and nature hikes, sports have long been a Camp Hollis tradition, and it all started with baseball.

Already a national pastime and an all-American sport by the 1940s, baseball caught the attention of Hollis leaders when they learned that a city in Pennsylvania had founded a new youth organization, Little League. Of course, kids had been playing sandlot ball for decades, but now there were uniforms and rules and championship games. When nearby Oswego formed its own Little League, Camp Hollis wanted in on the fun. To compete with other teams, Hollis staff created its own regulation-size ballfield.

Soon, baseball was part of camp's daily activities, with games played each afternoon. Campers who showed talent in the sport were given a spot on Hollis's official team, sometimes known as the "Camp Hollis 9"; at other times, they were the "Camp Hollis Boys." Camp Director Bob Bellinger noted its popularity: "Counselor Dave Geoway [1956–59] was our coach and usually after rest period there would be a ballgame. The whole camp would come down to watch the team and root for Camp Hollis."

A unique challenge for Coach Dave was the fact that his Hollis team had a whole new lineup every two weeks when a new group of campers arrived. But that didn't stop the ballplayers. Being on the Hollis team was an honor, and for a kid from an orphanage, like Craig Fisher, it remains a bright memory:

> When they were selecting members to be on the team, the coach asked, "Does anybody want to be a catcher?" I volunteered and ended up doing a pretty good job. After one game, a counselor asked me, "Who taught you how to catch? I like the way you handle the ball." I said that it was a Hollis counselor named Keith.

When Craig told me that story a few years ago, he couldn't remember much else about Keith, but archive records show that counselor was Keith Stroud, on staff in 1955 and '56, two of the years Craig attended. Keith's mentoring of the new Hollis catcher really made a difference for young

Fisher, who learned years later that he'd been featured several times on the *Palladium-Times'* sports page. He was headline news on August 6, 1956: "Murabito, Fisher Star for Camp 9." The reporter went on to say that "Craig Fisher, besides catching a magnificent game, drove in the deciding runs with a smashing double to right field. His tremendous ball handling was a big factor in the victory."

The Hollis team competed into the 1960s. When camp sessions changed from two weeks to one, however, there just wasn't enough time for sports directors to develop a competitive team. But they had plenty of other games for campers to enjoy. In fact, over the years, what qualifies as a camp-friendly sport has made for some unusual activities. For example, boxing.

After Judge Sullivan launched his new camp, he took time to film the historic events that shaped Hollis's early years. Included in footage of a typical camp day are boys donning boxing gloves, duking it out two by two. From the enthusiastic expressions on the campers circling the sparring boys, everybody wanted a turn. It appears that particular sport had a short history at Hollis, though. Other than the brief film clip, there is no other mention of boxing in the camp's archives.

Other Hollis sports activities are friendlier. Many children shoot their first arrow on the camp's archery range. Having strength to pull the bow's string back and let an arrow fly is a thrill—hitting the target is a bonus. The camp also introduces youth to volleyball and Frisbee golf, kids learn to dribble in high-speed basketball games like knockout and there have been endless variations of an obstacle course, which, along with a stopwatch, turns the Hollis playground into a challenge. By the early 1970s, along with the whole country, Camp Hollis had fallen in love with soccer. Soon, half the sports field became a sea of blue pinnies, the other half ablaze with yellow.

Sports can take over an entire camp session, especially when it's a Summer

"Camp...Hollis...is...GREAT!!!"

Olympics year. The sports director leads the Camp Hollis Olympics, and all week, campers prepare for the daylong competition. Each cabin adopts a country to represent and announces it with a large crayoned paper flag next to their front door. Finally, the tournament day arrives, kicked off by a counselor jogging across the sports field with a piece of driftwood aflame raised above their head, delivering Hollis's Olympic torch through a cheering

It's an exciting day when Camp Hollis holds its Olympics. The fun begins with a parade of countries represented in the sports contests. *Courtesy of the Camp Hollis Archives.*

crowd of campers. Then the activities begin: vinyl-covered mattresses are dragged from cabins, providing pole vaulters a soft landing; trails snaking through woods become courses for long-distance runners; and after heated competitions, the pool hosts relay races.

When the day is over, awards are presented, and counselors make sure that every camper is recognized for their efforts. But it isn't about winning—it's about being part of a team, a Camp Hollis philosophy that every sports director keeps in mind when planning activities: everyone participates. For kids who've been left out in gym class or on neighborhood playgrounds, Hollis has always been a place where you get a chance.

After two or three morning activities, stomachs are grumbling. But before enjoying Lunch, campers head for the bathrooms, where they crowd around sinks to soap away the morning sweat and dirt. Then, two lines form at the entrances to the dining hall, and campers try to get a good look at what's on

the table. More good food, more refills on milk and, now and then, a new dessert to try. Counselor Joanie Koster Mayhew explained how "some kids were afraid to eat Jello because it moved."

———∿∿∿———

One way or another, everyone's belly gets filled, which makes what comes next a real treat. Campers call it REST PERIOD, but to the staff, it's "a counselor's favorite activity." With a nod to the siesta, rest period is a one-hour respite from the heat of the day. It's a time to write letters home,* read or work on a boondoggle. But for most counselors, it's the perfect opportunity to catch forty winks. Alarm clocks are essential because rest period can easily turn into rest afternoon, and for kids, there's more fun just waiting to happen.

———∿∿∿———

Two more activity periods start out the afternoon, giving each camper a chance to get a daily dose of sports, Arts & Crafts, nature, swimming and a few other camp favorites. By 3:00 p.m. or so, with two hours remaining before supper, staff are challenged to come up with unique ways to ease into evening. In Hollis's early years, the whole camp would head to the lake for one last refreshing dip. When swimming shifted from lake to pool, the camp

---

* In the camp's early years, staff handed out penny postcards, ensuring that every camper wrote a note home. Counselors screened those messages, on the lookout for kids with a bad case of homesickness.

would split into two groups, each taking a turn cooling off while the other hung out under the playground's shade trees.

In recent years, campers participate in the daily activities by traveling in groups formed from various cabins, making late afternoon the perfect opportunity for kids to get to know their bunkmates. CABIN GROUP TIME made sense; smaller groups of campers felt more like family or, you might say, tribes. Back in the 1960s and '70s, the small groups were given Native American names: Sioux, Mohawks, Apache and so on. Counselors introduced a little folklore about their specific tribe or inspired pride by creating chants and songs.

A first Cabin Group Time activity might be learning everyone's name. Counselors then find out if their group is into basketball or hiking or braiding hair. Whatever the group is in the mood for becomes that day's Cabin Group Time activity. It's a bonding experience, one that has grown in importance as families back home have become busier and are often fragmented.

―――

As the afternoon winds down, everybody's ready for more food. While breakfast is often bowls of cereal and lunch is sandwiches and chips, SUPPER is a full-course meal. Through camp's long history, favorites emerge. The kitchen can always count on requests for seconds and thirds of spaghetti with homemade sauce or chicken cooked on the grill. In the 1990s, staff named that grilled meat "stinky pigeon," and counselor Adam DeMott (2001, '04, '06) remembered a chant the whole camp yelled during that meal: "What the? Who the? Stinky pigeon, I really wanna chew ya!" Many suppers were a cause for celebration, even a hot dog roast served at the picnic area or on the beach. It isn't just good food that makes Hollis meals so special—it's how those meals are served.

Like a scene out of *The Waltons*, Camp Hollis's dining hall has always been set up family style. Long tables welcome a dozen or so campers—girls on one side and boys on the other. Once seated, campers get a close-up view of what's in large bowls, with tempting aromas drifting up and down the tables. But no one gets their first bite until a blessing is offered and the people sitting at each end of the table—the counselors—begin serving.

From the head of those tables, counselors take on the role of moms and dads. Though often only a few years older than campers, counselors are trusted with the important job of making sure everyone gets fed until full.

Hollis staff member J.J. Wheeler (1989–96) uses a Camp Hollis tradition to make an announcement in the dining hall. *Courtesy of the Camp Hollis Archives.*

For many boys and girls, especially those from orphanages or broken homes, someone paying attention to them makes mealtime special. The dining hall often starts off quiet, with only the sound of spoons and forks scraping plates. Then a counselor starts a conversation—"Anybody hit the bull's-eye in archery today?"—and soon the hall reverberates with stories and laughter. Without fail, the camp director or kitchen manager interrupts the clatter—their raised hand signals everyone to raise theirs and stop talking—and reminds the camp to keep conversation at a reasonable level. The quiet returns for a minute or two, but the volume steadily climbs back up, often with added enthusiasm.

⟞⟋⟍⟍⟍⟞

After a generous dessert and a song or two, the action-packed day continues with FREE TIME, which counselor Patty Maxon (1974–77) described as "any three kids could grab a counselor to do what they most wanted to do." It might be more Arts & Crafts, another hike or a pickup game of basketball. In the days before mandatory recycling, kids headed down to the beach to look for sea glass: tiny treasures formed when bottles were tossed into Lake Ontario, where they broke into pieces and were smoothed by years of stormy weather. Sea glass were prized collectibles, with greens the most common and reds or blues a rare gem.

—⁓⁓⁓—

While campers enjoy this Free Time, a few counselors set up for the final event of the day, NIGHT ACTIVITY. This all-camp activity didn't start out needing a lot of planning. Early in Hollis's history, counselors led a long nightly hike that ended at the lake. There everybody grabbed a piece of driftwood for the evening campfire. For decades, Night Activity took place at the "Center of the Sun," a mowed area on the nearby Salvatore's Grove/ Nunzi's property. Dave Canfield (camp director, 1987, and Youth Bureau supervisor, 1988–89) remembered the activities at the Grove:

> There was enough room for an all-camp soccer game or maybe blog tag. We even had evening snack there or spent time watching the sun set. But Center of the Sun always ended with a trip down Tumble Hill, a gentle slope where kids and counselors loved the dizzy feeling you got when you reached the bottom.

If rain ruined the outdoor evening plans, Judge Sullivan would borrow a projector to run two-reel 8mm Tom Mix and Hopalong Cassidy movies, a form of entertainment most campers in the '40s and '50s hadn't experienced. If there wasn't a movie to show, groups could gather around the fireplace for

a game of "Killer." Hours were spent trying to figure out who the winking murderer was.

As time went on, counselors planning Night Activity looked beyond hikes and movies for their inspiration. A 1969 end-of-season report by Camp Director Joe Rotolo (1968–69) listed evening programs that suggest his staff liked sending campers on a hunt. The report mentioned scavenger hunts, "most interesting rock" hunts, a junk hunt and even a hunt for bubblegum. But the best hunt of all still takes place at least once every Hollis season: Counselor Hunt. Staff love that hunt because they get to hide anywhere in the mowed area of the campgrounds or up to ten feet into the woods. Smart counselors grab a green army blanket and blend into tall grass and shrubs, giving them an hour of peace while campers keep hunting.

By the 1980s, sports-minded counselors invented a new Night Activity called Border Patrol, a high-energy running game played on the full length of the field. After being divided into two groups, campers and staff are sent to opposite ends of the field. The leader yells a category—"Everyone wearing red—run!" "If you had three helpings of dinner tonight—run!"— and those in that category would hightail it, attempting to make it to the other side without being tagged. In the middle of the field were a few designated taggers who could freeze runners with a single touch. Those unlucky statues could only be unfrozen by a teammate. Border Patrol tends to get heated (especially for counselors who don't like losing), and there's bound to be a few head-on collisions. Camp nurses learn to ask if it's a Border Patrol night; if so, she makes sure there are plenty of icepacks in the freezer.

Other Night Activities are determined by the weather, like when Oswego County is in the middle of a heat wave. Depending on the era, the entire camp either heads to the lake or the pool for a cooling evening of relay races and "biggest splash" or "worst belly flop" contests. (Winners are determined by the loudest cheers.) Occasionally, a lifeguard adds some suspense by climbing atop the pool house and diving into the deep end. Much safer, but still fun, were the greased watermelon contests held in the lake—camper Linda Jessmore claims she can still smell the grease. The entire camp was divided into two teams that attempted to push the bobbing fruit to a buoy finish line. Win or lose, everybody got a slice of the prize.

There are comical Night Activities like Kangaroo Court, a mock trial complete with a robed judge and three bizarrely dressed jurors. Campers and counselors accused of some wrongdoing (most "crimes" were fabricated) are called in front of the whole group and found not guilty or, heaven help them, guilty. One never knows what the punishment will be: serving a counselor their meals for a day, one hundred pushups on the ballfield, getting a raw egg cracked on a bare head…and those are the milder punishments.

To help create memorable Night Activities, the camp keeps a dress-up box filled with costumes and props. Counselors rummage through it to give themselves dramatic makeovers, becoming superheroes or fairy tale characters. Sometimes campers are put in charge of the transformation in an activity known as "Dress Your Counselor Night." Kim Kedenburg (2001–3) recalled how her campers worked on her. "When they got done, I would have made Frankenstein's wife look like a supermodel. Campers took my hair, which came down to my elbows, and teased it straight up with 100 pounds of hairspray. Then they filled that with as many dead leaves as they could find. It took me three days to get the hairspray and leaves out of my hair, but the shocked and awed looks from the kids were fantastic!"

Some Night Activities are such a major part of the Hollis program that counselors devote a whole camp session to them. During Carnival Week, each day's games and projects drop hints of the big night, slowly building expectations. When the event finally arrives, visitors to Camp Hollis might think they're at an actual carnival. Counselors are dressed like clowns and fortune tellers. There's fun food to "purchase" with tickets the campers are given or can earn at games of chance. A popular Carnival attraction is the marriage booth, where campers tie the knot with their favorite counselor—or counselors, if they're experiencing multiple crushes. Pipe cleaner wedding rings seal the deal.

Although these popular activities are usually dreamed up by staff—more examples of memorable Night Activities can be found in the chapter "It's A Camp Hollis Tradition!"—sometimes inspiration comes from campers. That was the case for one Night Activity that Jeff Von Wald (1993–97, '99) created:

One summer, another counselor and I were talking about how many kids seemed more interested in video games than camp activities. So we decided to try to make a popular video game into a live activity. Neither of us knew much about those games, so we interviewed a camper who was really into them. He described the characters and challenges of his favorite game, Super Mario Brothers. From that, we made a rotation of activities that paralleled the various stages the video game went through, including diving for treasures in the pool, being chased by birds and turtles, and ultimately knocking out "King Koopa" by hitting him 100 times with dodgeballs. King Koopa was played by [counselor] Pat Sheffield [1990–96] dressed in catcher's equipment.

By the end of Night Activity, the sun has either slid into the lake or is just about to. But the long day of activities isn't over. After heading back to the dorms or cabins and grabbing a sweatshirt, clusters of kids, led by their counselor, make their way to CAMPFIRE. Some years, circling around the roaring flames was a nightly event. Back then, Camp Hollis neighbors learned to accept their summer days ending with one hundred voices singing at top volume.

Every five years or so, a new collection of favorite songs rings out from Lewis's Bluff. Depending on the era, campers learn the words and hand motions to "Desperado," "Three Jolly Fisherman," "John Jacob Jingleheimer-Schmidt," "Blowin' in the Wind," "The Cruel War," "I've Got Six Pence," "Boom Chicka Boom," "Shoo Shoo Fly Pie," "The Princess Pat," "Little Red Wagon," "The Bear Song," "If I Weren't at This Camp" or "Baby Shark." Campers are quick learners, and those songs end up being sung morning, noon and night. By summer's end, counselors never want to hear them again.

Camp Hollis has been the subject of several original songs. There's "The Hollis Clap," which, decades later, former campers and staff can still clap in perfect rhythm. There's "Hollis Will Shine," credited to counselor Jean Galvin (1953), who composed this optimistic lyric:

> *Hollis will shine tonight, Hollis will shine*
> *All down the line tonight, Hollis will shine*
> *We're all dressed up tonight*
> *Don't we look fine*
> *When the sun goes down and the moon comes up*
> *Hollis will shine!*

Not to be outdone, the 2006 staff came up with their own song—a repeat-after-me chant, actually. It's "The Camp Hollis Spirit":

> *I got the Camp Hollis spirit*
> *I got it all the time*
> *Gonna pick it on up*
> *and pass it along*
> *to my good friend* _____ [the name of a counselor or camper is
> sung and he or she repeats the song]

The song can go on five or more minutes; fun at first, but it gets old real fast.

The Fisher children, who were raised in the Oswego Children's Home, loved the 1950s campfire songs. When writing his camp memories, Frank noted how "those songs still come to mind. There was "Found a Peanut," "Who Threw the Overalls in Mrs. Murphy's Chowder" and "The Cow Kicked Nelly in the Belly in the Barn." Frank's sister, Christine, never forgot the joke in one song. "It was about the United States and began, 'Oh where has Ora gone, boys, Oh where has Ora gone? I ask you again as a personal friend, Where has Ora gone?' And the response, 'She's gone to the Merry Land, boys,' and on and on until we had exhausted our state name resources."

Sometimes a song heard at Hollis becomes a faint memory, and the desire to hear it again can be strong. That's true for me with a song I remember from my camper years. I was pretty sure I knew the title, "The Cannibal King," and although I could still hear its bouncing melody, its words escaped me. I asked the right person when I mentioned the song to Frank Fisher; he was able to recite it word for word, starting with the correct title:

> *"The Mighty King"*
> *Oh, the Mighty King with a big gold ring*
> *fell in love with a lusty maiden*
> *And every night in the pale moon light*
> *across the lake he came*
>
> *A hug and a kiss for the pretty little miss*
> *in the shade of the bamboo tree*
> *And every night in the pale moon light*
> *it sounded like this to me-e-e*
>
> *Barump (kiss kiss), barump (kiss kiss),*
> *barump body ahdi ay ayay*
> *Barump (kiss kiss), barump (kiss kiss),*
> *barump body ahdi ay ayay*

Those campfire songs have a way of becoming lodged in our minds, as does the memory of the counselors who led them. In my camper days, counselor Bill Noun (1968–69) made a lasting impression on me. At the time, Bill was a student at Oswego State and a talented musician who'd serenade us with a ukulele. Bill shared popular folk songs at campfire, and if we didn't know their words when we arrived at camp, we sure did before we left. Bill made it a point to single out lyrics that he thought had special meaning to Camp Hollis, like the song "Home on the Range."

"The next song I'm gonna sing," Bill would say, strumming his uke, "is one you already know, but its words are very important, so listen carefully." "Home, home on the range," he'd start, "where the deer and the antelope play." Pausing, Bill pointed to his ear. "Where seldom is heard a discouraging word…." To make sure we were listening, he repeated that line, this time slowly. Fifty years later, I still believe what Bill Noun taught us: Camp Hollis has always been built by its leaders' encouraging words.

Intermingled with those memorable songs are skits, way way way off-Broadway theatrics performed by a more-than-willing staff. Each new group of campers learns "The Legend of George Hollis" (described in the "It's a Camp Hollis Tradition!" chapter), and depending on if the camp director thought scaring kids was okay, there might be a ghost story or two. There were also cornball skits like "Mr. Catch-It-All," where a counselor enters a doctor's office with a stomachache and proceeds to pick up every other illness in the waiting room; "Purple Pancakes," in which a movie director keeps changing how the cast acts out their painful deaths from eating poisoned pancakes; or "J.C. Penney," where, one by one, counselors show off a new article of clothing, mentioning they got theirs from J.C. Penney. The skit concludes when a counselor, barely covered by a towel, runs past the campers yelling "Help! Somebody stole my clothes! I'm J.C. Penney!" Campers fall off their fire circle seats laughing, but in truth, it's the counselors having the most fun.

Now and then, Hollis is lucky enough to have a trained storyteller on staff. Eric Hunn (2003–4) brought his award-winning talents to the camp. Back when Eric was in fourth grade, he claimed first prize in an Oswego County storytelling contest with his rendition of *Strega Nona*. Eric has this advice for staff who make an appearance on the Hollis campfire "stage": "The job of counselor often requires you to be a bit of a performer. Being able to tell stories helps with that a lot."

With memorable songs and skits, Camp Hollis campfires continue to shine years after experiencing them. Here's how Christine Fisher recalled those special times:

> *There's something mesmerizing and perfect about a campfire on the beach, sitting on the rocks and adjusting a blanket or sweater for warmth and comfort. And there's something about my very first toasted marshmallow. A wee white lump fixed to the end of a stick and held over or in a fire and lifted out aflame! Oh, how I loved the burnt crust with the goo dripping*

Children gathered at a campfire never know which songs and stories they'll hear from the Hollis counselors. *Courtesy of the Camp Hollis Archives.*

from the middle. There were songs, of course, and there was silence as we sat and watched the fire burn down, only the sound of lake on rocks as background.

As campfire nears its end, attention shifts to the western horizon. No one needs to be told why. Even if it's a camper's first Lake Ontario sunset, they know they're witnessing something sacred. For maybe the only time during a day of camp activities, in the three or four minutes it takes the blazing sun to disappear, all are unified in silence.

Counselors have learned to end campfire with quiet, slow songs, a musical message to campers that bedtime is approaching. For decades, the song of choice was "Kumbaya," with its mesmerizing hand motions. More recently, "The Eagle Song" provides a meditation on the wonders of living close to nature:

Have you all seen the eagle
flying so high
encircling the universe
on the wings of pure light…

———〰———

With the campgrounds now in total darkness, groups of children stick close to their counselor and head for FLAG LOWERING. Forming a silent circle, young and old break the quiet, raising their voices:

> *Day is done*
> *Gone the sun*
> *From the lakes from the hills from the sky*
> *All is well*
> *Safely rest*
> *God is nigh.*

A counselor ceremoniously lowers the flag as another gathers it before it touches the ground. Then the two leaders neatly fold the flag, military style, signaling the end of another day at Camp Hollis. On particularly peaceful nights, the camp director might keep the group in a circle a few more minutes. With little artificial light, campers can witness an undisturbed night sky. After a few announcements about Polar Bear Swim and a hint or two about the next day's activities, group by group, campers head off to BEDTIME.

———〰———

One might assume that after a long day of outdoor fun, children would be anxious to climb into their bunks and drift into a peaceful sleep. But camp counselors will correct that misconception; in fact, they may tell you that bedtime is the toughest hour of supervising children. After giving their all since early morning and having had one forty-five-minute break, counselors just want to relax, hang out with the staff and raid the kitchen for snacks. But none of that can happen until they deal with children sharing a bedroom with a bunch of new friends.

Tips on putting kids to bed have been traded between staff since the first year of camp on Lewis's Bluff. Counselor and site director Pat Cloonan explained how he figured out Camp Hollis's bedtime routine:

> *I remember the hard time we had getting the campers to go to sleep in the dorms. We'd keep telling them it was time to stop talking and get some rest, but*

Why is Robby's bunk covered with letters from his family?

He was homesick. This seemed like the best cure.

they kept gabbing. Finally, I decided to try reading to my campers. I found some chapter books that were good for their age level and we counselors took turns reading a chapter a night. It worked great to get the kids to calm down and go to sleep.

More recently, workshops at the staff's pre-camp training cover effective methods of getting kids to settle in for the night. A major topic in those workshops addresses the biggest challenge for many attending an overnight camp: homesickness.

Considered a rite of passage, surviving homesickness is how children begin to gain independence, and that first step often happens at a sleepaway camp. Going away to camp prepares them for future goodbyes, whether it be heading off to college, moving out of a childhood home or, as it was for camper Richard Allen House, "getting ready to go into the military." Some children easily adjust to camp's home away from home. For others, going to camp is a big step—too big for a few. Counselors expend a lot of energy helping homesick children. It's a day-by-day (sometimes hour-by-hour) process. Campers struggling the most—the ones who don't seem to be overcoming their homesickness—become important to counselors. Just ask John Baumann:

> *I would do everything in my power to cajole the camper into not calling his parents. "No One Leaves" was my mantra, and what I meant was, no one gives up if I can help it. On that first night, each camper knew someone friendly was watching out for them. Some of this I learned from our director, Judy McManus, who wanted us to try to make the children comfortable and not just send them home right away.*

Creating that supportive atmosphere at bedtime, when homesickness is often at its worst, requires counselors to establish enjoyable routines: ten minutes of chat time before lights out, reading or making up a story on the spot or serenading campers with a quiet song on guitar. If all goes well, counselors begin hearing campers giving in to sleep, their rhythmic breathing or snoring creating a chorus one by one. Finally, exhausted counselors tiptoe outside, take a seat on the steps and meet up with other staff. Those few minutes of peace are a small reward for providing kids another nonstop day of Camp Hollis fun.

IT'S A CAMP HOLLIS TRADITION!

It may seem odd to begin a chapter covering Camp Hollis traditions with stories about the weather, but the skies over Lewis's Bluff have been "raining down" memorable occasions since the camp first opened. With a neighbor like Lake Ontario churning up storms on a regular basis, every summer promises to give campers and counselors something to write home about. Director Dave Canfield was eyewitness to a storm's lightning bolt that bounced off a car in the parking lot. That storm passed quickly, but Dave had to deal with what the lightning left behind: "The power line that ran from the well at the bluff to the main building had been knocked out, leaving the camp without water."

Camp leaders learn to always keep their eye on the weather. Director Rick Pawlewicz (1994–95) also found himself in the middle of an unusually powerful storm. On what appeared to be a quiet summer evening at Hollis, Lake Ontario had other ideas, causing Rick to say, "It will go down in Camp Hollis history and into my mind's vault of unforgettable experiences." Here's his story:

> The weather had taken its toll on Camp Hollis and the counselors. Temperatures soared well into the triple digits on a daily basis and humid nights made for almost unsleepable conditions. It was Friday night, the end of the last full day before campers would return home. As the night drifted into early Saturday morning, a light breeze came up and it was incredibly comforting. Then, the sound of thunder drew me to the patio off the main

building. I was greeted by Robin Emond [1992–96], the Evening Security Guard, who patrolled the grounds. It was the end of his shift, but, for no particular reason, Robin stayed a little later. We sat and watched the beautiful display of "God-like fingers" falling from the sky.

The thunder became louder and the lightning brighter and more frequent. Robin and I instinctively took off to warn the counselors and campers. Within minutes, the light breeze turned into large gales and the sky filled with rain. At this point, only five or six cabins had been warned, but Robin and I continued on to the remaining bunks. By this time, the rain had turned to hail, traveling almost horizontally.

I came to Cabin 4 (I'd worked my way back from 12) and the wind was too intense for me to remain outside. I slipped into the doorway (there was no way to fully open it because the wind was too strong) and told everyone to get under their beds and put their pillows over their heads. Just as counselors Antoinette Nelson [1991–96] and Margaret Kaiser [1993, '95] made their way under their cots, a window began to detach from the cabin structure. An explosion of glass seemed to alleviate the cabin pressure and, a few minutes later, the winds subsided.

Rick estimated that the entire storm lasted between five and fifteen minutes. He then recruited a few counselors to walk the grounds and assess the damage. What they found was a path of destruction starting from the lakeshore that traveled through the camp and ended at Cabin 4 before heading into the woods. Although officials from the National Weather Service never confirmed what happened that night at Camp Hollis, Rick is convinced it was a wind shear, a tornado-like storm that carves a distinctive pathway.

Also on staff that summer was Jim Hooper, the camp's nature director. Jim got soaking wet when Rick opened his cabin door to warn about the storm, but being a true nature enthusiast, he used the meteorological event as a teachable moment:

The next morning, I formed a 100-person nature hike around the campgrounds. We saw windows sucked into cabins, trees down, and garbage cans tossed from outside the main building. We also found a canoe that had been tacoed—bent in half. There were cinder blocks of the pool house that had been raised up.

Jim tried to process what he was seeing while calming campers and helping them appreciate the awesome display of nature they were witnessing. Then he noticed a tree near his cabin that had come down during the storm. Aware that he'd witnessed a once-in-a-lifetime event, Jim got an idea of how to preserve his memory of that night. "I cut one of the tree's branches off with my Swiss Army knife and made a hiking stick. I still carry it with me wherever I go."

Memorable Camp Hollis events also take place in the absence of storms, when summer feels tropical day and night. During those dry spells, counselors have to throw out their plans and think wet. Those times, Pat Fink (2013–15) believes, are "what makes camp so special. It's how you learn to respond to those curveballs." Pat offered an example of staff ingenuity that happened during his "hottest summer at Hollis":

> It started with a broken pool filter that lasted for weeks. However, rather than mope about the heat, the staff took up the challenge and worked water into every activity. Kids were jumping from slip-and-slide obstacle courses to water balloon wars. Finally, the pool was to open back up. Temperatures were high 90s all week and we planned to reopen the pool with Thursday's night activity: a synchronized swimming competition. My campers dove headlong into the contest, our whole cabin becoming wildly tightknit, practicing at odd hours, creating solos for each camper, and guarding their secret choreography from other cabins. Then, on competition day, the campers chose to march single-file around camp to intimidate the other cabins until it was show time. Ten kids got into the shallow end of the pool, we hit play and "Wannabe" by the Spice Girls blared. The team danced their heart out, and each camper got their chance to lead. I don't remember if the competition had a winner or not, but I know we had an awesome time.

Aside from an occasional weather event, counselors' activities usually go as planned. The most successful of these become camp traditions, and like every organization, Hollis thrives on them. Some last five or ten years, long enough for a generation to call them their own. Others carry on for decades, allowing campers from the 1960s to trade stories with their counterparts from fifty years later. A few traditions have, remarkably, managed to cover Hollis's entire history. But whether short-lived or enduring, traditions only hang on if they're needed. Consider the origins of a popular Hollis tradition from the 1960s known as Red & White Teams.

After years of running camp the same way, staff were looking for new activities to keep campers motivated and enthusiastic. They wanted something boys and girls could work toward together, unlike the individual goals of passing a swim test or hitting the bull's-eye. This new incentive would need to inspire the whole group and be exciting enough to maintain campers' interest for their entire two-week stay. Finally, counselors wanted something simple enough for children to understand—as simple as, say, knowing red from white.

Here's how this competition of colors worked. Once a new group of campers passed their health checks and found a bunk, they were equally divided into teams of red and white. Counselors hung an appropriately colored wooden nametag around campers' necks, proclaiming each boy and girl "red" or "white." Counselors were similarly divided and led their team in a variety of games and challenges, accumulating points for each win.

Red/white activities could show up anytime during the day: in the middle of a swim or halfway through lunch. They became the focus of many night activities, such as Capture the Flag. Chants of "I'd rather be dead than red!" could be heard while swift runners earned points for their team and a gold star on their nametag.

One way to add big points to a color's team involved hiding and finding a piece of driftwood that, with a splash of color, became a symbol of superiority. It was known as the Kohanna stick and was originally created by Camp Director Joe Rotolo, who, in 1969, painted the stick, which he described as an Indian war club, with red and white rings. Whichever color group had possession of the Kohanna was obligated to show it at least once a day, choosing a time when all campers were gathered together and could witness the showing. Some lucky kid got to rush out of the woods, swinging the stick over his or her head yelling "Kohanna! Kohanna! Kohanna!" (It was vital that the name was screamed three, and only three, times.) The camper then ran back into the woods and, with the help of his or

"I say we wave the white flag on this one."

her counselors, rehid the Kohanna—making sure that a certain number of the color stripes were showing—thus tempting the other team to drop everything and take up the hunt.

To make finding the Kohanna even more challenging, opposing teams would hide a series of written clues, often sending the other team on a wild goose chase. As the stick went back and forth from red to white, points added up and the hiding intensified. In fact, sometimes campers got so good at hiding the stick that they forgot where they'd put it. For days there were no showings, until someone beat down the tall grass to uncover it.

The Red & White competition continued until the last day of camp, when final scores were totaled and the winner was announced at lunch. After finishing their last meal before heading home, the losing team had a traditional dessert—an apple or a cookie—while the winners celebrated with a dish of ice cream.

Traditions like Red & White focused on being part of a group, but Camp Hollis also has rituals for singling out people. Anyone lucky enough to be at camp on their birthday receives special treatment—in a one-of-a-kind way. It starts at the end of a meal with a rousing version of "Happy Birthday to You," then quickly escalates to the full camp chanting "Skip Around the Room! Skip Around the Room! Won't Shut Up 'Til You Skip Around the Room!" As the chant promises, the yelling does not end until the reluctant birthday honoree leaves his or her seat and circles the dining hall, skipping all the way.

Mealtime is also time for the tradition of Singing for the Mail. Letters from home have always been cherished by both campers and counselors; this was especially true before cellphones and the internet changed how we stay connected. A letter from a loved one is a link to your other life, but before anyone reads their news from home, they must sing—in front of the entire camp. Since the soloist gets to choose any song they want, many take the easy way out and offer "Twinkle Twinkle Little Star."

Camp Hollis traditions are often a result of children thoroughly enjoying certain activities. If it was fun one summer, kids expect it the next. Counselors make note of those popular activities and create themes to expand on them. Themes are often based on holidays, such as Christmas or the Fourth of July; one holiday really got counselors' creative juices flowing. Jim Hooper described how the Hollis staff made a memorable celebration of Halloween:

While a party with games and snacks was going on in the dining hall, we turned the old Arts & Crafts building into a haunted house. Staff knew ahead of time what week we'd be celebrating Halloween and we talked it up all summer, with each counselor trying to come up with the most frightening character or situation. One summer, I was up in rafters and as campers came through, I'd try to grab them. Another summer, I appeared as just a head on a platter.

Counselors Antoinette Nelson (1991–96) and Tom Marsallo (1991–93) "serve up" Christy Germain (1991–93) at Hollis's Halloween haunted house. *Courtesy of the Camp Hollis Archives.*

Indeed, counselors came up with many frightening characters that became their Halloween alter egos. There were the standard witches and devils, but some staff looked beyond the obvious to elicit camper screams. Brent Jones became a patient whose surgery had gone bad. Laid atop a table, with cooked spaghetti piled on his stomach, Brent moaned that his guts were coming out. Jeff Von Wald went for offbeat humor by turning into a monster who startled kids by jumping out from behind a curtain and yelling, "Eat your vegetables!"

Lots of children looked forward to the annual scare-a-thon. It helped that counselors made sure that campers understood the horror was all in good fun. "We always set it up so only children who wanted to go through the house would do so," Jeff said. Then, when it was all over, before the haunted house was turned back into the Arts & Crafts building, counselors turned on the lights and walked campers through a second time, giving them the chance to see their counselors smiling beneath makeup and costumes, letting them in on the joke.

Over the years, how Halloween is celebrated in schools and communities has raised concerns for parents. As costumes got scarier and pranks became riskier, Camp Hollis has shifted how the holiday is celebrated. In 2013, Brandon Morey (2011–16), who oversaw the Hollis program through his Youth Bureau position, initiated a new camp tradition, known as Hollis Harvest:

> *I'd brought my family to the Ontario Orchards Fall Festival and thought it would be fun to provide a safe, family-friendly fall-themed event at Camp Hollis. We planned activities on the main field, food and drinks in the dining hall, walks on the trails, pumpkin carving in the Arts & Crafts building and camp staff in cabins so kids could trick-or-treat in costume. We anticipated a decent turnout, but we were not prepared when between 200 and 300 people attended. We ran out of candy in less than 20 minutes.*
>
> *The next year we thought we were more prepared. Local agencies and organizations "sponsored" cabins by decorating them and providing their own treats. A few local farms donated pumpkins and food. Volunteers helped with activities and parking. The second year we had over 1,000 people and we still ran out of candy, activities and food, but everybody— kids and parents—loved it.*

Traditions like the haunted house at Hollis happened each summer for a decade or two, which is small potatoes compared to an event that, for nearly fifty years, took place on the last night of each camp session. From the 1940s into the '90s, counselors planned a dance called the Hollis Hop, a celebration featuring current hit songs, special refreshments for snack and, in the early years of the camp, an awards ceremony. Along with certificates for the camp's best archer and swimmer, a royal treatment was bestowed on one boy and girl each session. Those lucky youngsters—the camp queen and king—were escorted to their thrones (wooden chairs covered with red construction paper) and then crowned with aluminum foil tiaras.

Throughout the camp session, excitement for the Hollis Hop intensified. By the afternoon of the dance, it was all that was on everyone's mind. Counselor Cindy Czerow Nacey remembered the Hollis Hop "as a big deal. The girls would bring their best clothes—some had pretty petticoats—from home. We'd help them get dressed up and they would be so excited." Marie Bailey was a camper in the late 1940s, and she mentioned the kindness of those female counselors as the girls prepared for the dance. "They took rags to do up our hair in curls. I didn't really need that help since my hair was naturally curly, but I did it anyway."

As a camper in the 1960s, I witnessed an example of that counselor kindness and remembered it into my adulthood, prompting me to write a poem I called "Some Enchanted Evening":

The girl counselors gave her a pair of white gloves
two of its fingers
filled with tissue painted flesh-brown
to hold the place
where her two fingers would have slid in
had she had them.

It was the talk of the camp at the dance
a little lesson in kindness
that was whispered ear to ear
adding mystery
to my first dance.

From the bench against the dining hall wall
I watched her
in her simple Cinderella dress:
hair brushed and ribboned
giggling with her best camp friend and
all evening long
offering her confident hand
in dance.

Over in the boys' dorm, getting ready for the Hollis Hop was a whole different ball of wax. Counselor Mike McCrobie (1975) described the pre-dance scene:

We male counselors would bring a bottle of "vintage" cologne or aftershave to camp each week. I didn't do much shaving as a 17-year-old, but I do recall cleaning out my dad's medicine cabinet to bring in bottles of Brut, English Leather and Hai Karate that I'm pretty sure had been fermenting since LBJ was president. In a rite of passage, the young boys would cup their hands and splash on the masculine colognes. Like Macaulay Culkin depicted years later in the box office hit Home Alone, *there were lots of peach-fuzzed cheeks stinging as they splashed on Aqua Velva or Old Spice for the first time.*

Imagine the doors to the dining-room-turned-dance-hall-for-the-evening opening and 40–50 prepubescent boys strutting into the room, sporting a mixture of aromatic fragrances from days gone by. I don't know what a French brothel smells like, but I'm willing to bet that it may have smelled something like the Friday night Hollis Hops of 1975.

Those hair-styled girls and fragrant boys were in for a surprise when they stepped into the Camp Hollis dining hall. Among the secrets kept about the big event was the theme for the dance. Counselors dreamed those up, and John Baumann recalled the memorable ones from his 1980s Hollis summers:

There was a Country Hop, with a cowboy theme and a Halloween Hop, which was a costume Hop. Once a summer we had our '50s theme. The movie Grease *was popular at the time, so the boys slicked back their hair and dressed in white T-shirts with something rolled in their sleeve to look like a pack of cigarettes. Girls had their hair done up and were in hoop skirts. Everybody walked around in groups with an attitude.*

To set the proper mood for the theme, counselors brought props from home and raided the Arts & Crafts building for crepe paper, turning the familiar dining hall into a magical scene. One of 1957's themes, "Teahouse on the August Moon," replaced standard light bulbs hung from the ceiling with oriental lanterns. In the early '90s, Disney movies like *The Little Mermaid* sent the hall "Under the Sea." And when disco was the rage in the 1970s, glitter was the go-to decoration, including a spinning, sparkling ball hanging from a rafter. The kitchen staff created a disco dessert when the Hop's theme was *Soul Train*, rolling out a large train-shaped cake to "oohs" and "aahs."

Judge Eugene and Mrs. Ruth Sullivan, special guests at a Camp Hollis Hop, dance to the delight of the campers. *Courtesy of the Sullivan family.*

Although most of the Hop themes were planned by the female staff, one summer in the 1960s, the guy counselors decided to try their hand at the Beatles-themed "Norwegian Wood." As staff person Pat Cloonan explained, "We decorated the dining hall with lots of tree branches from the woods." Pat also remembered that one

"Buddy Holly, Mama Cass and Chuck Berry!
They never miss a Hollis Hop."

of his jobs at the Hop was "to make sure the kids who hadn't been asked to dance got a chance to do so."

Pat and other counselors would have found those shy kids sitting on benches lined up along the walls, boys on one side of the room and girls on the other. Some wondered if they'd sit there the whole night, but a friendly counselor, or sometimes the music, had a way of winning over even the most shy. In the camp's early years, a small hi-fi atop the fireplace mantel handled the evening's soundtrack. Later, a stereo system was rigged up in the kitchen, where a counselor playing deejay sent the latest hits to huge speakers in the dining hall. For many campers, those songs are markers of their first social event.

"I learned to dance at the Hollis Hop," said William Dickerson. "From that point on, I fancied myself quite an amazing jitter bugger." Frank Fisher not only had his first dance at the Hop, but he also worked up the nerve to ask someone to be his partner:

> *A female counselor noticed me sitting against the wall, shy and afraid, but trying not to show it. She came over and sat with me a moment, then took my hand and walked me out on the floor. I held back a little, saying "I don't know how." She smiled and laughed quietly without laughing at me and explained "You don't have to. Just shuffle your feet without stepping." Soon we were slow dancing.*
>
> *I don't know how she knew, but when the dance finished, she walked me over to a young redheaded camper for whom I did have a crush. The counselor said to me "I know you like _____, so dance." She put our hands together and gently pushed us out on the dance floor. We talked and danced until the end of the Hop when "Goodnight Irene, Goodnight Irene, I'll see you in my dreams" had ended.*

Those slow dances sometimes ended with something even more memorable: camper Nora Carson remembered that at her 1970s-era Hollis Hop, "I had my first kiss."

Hollis Hops changed over the years, reflecting the shift in how young people socialized. By the 1980s, rather than dancing as couples, campers

118

For many campers, the Hollis Hop was their introduction to social events, which included the excitement of dancing with someone special. *Courtesy of the Camp Hollis Archives.*

congregated in groups. And the hits during that era weren't all sunshine and lollipops. John Baumann remembered the music being "dark":

> *They were sluggish, synth-based dance-pop: thump-schwack, thump thump-schwack. Still, those silly sounds occasionally lifted us into a transcendent unity, 100 campers all doing "The Safety Dance," or a line dance to Men at Work's "Land Down Under." It was Forrest LaBarre who introduced us to "The Forrest Dance," a simple dance step perfect for anyone too shy to get up and boogie or too scattered to remember steps.*

John mentioned one detail about Hollis Hop dances that didn't add to the celebration. "What I've almost forgotten in this age of air conditioning is how hot it was in that building during those dances. All the doors and windows would be open, all the fans blasting, and it would still be 90-something sweltering degrees. But we danced like we were shaking off $50 bills."

It's hard to compete with those Hollis Hop memories, but there is one tradition that's been around even longer than the dance party. Ever since Camp Hollis counselors have tried to figure out how to entertain kids, they've told ghost stories. And not just your standard spooky legend, like

"The Man with the Golden Arm" or "The Flying Dutchman." When it comes to creating a scary story, Hollis counselors excel. Here's an example from staff members Foster Caffrey (2005, 2008–9) and Shaun Del Rosario (2005, 2008–9), who managed to come up with a real whopper.

"As a reward on the last night of camp," Shaun explained, "we told our campers that if they were mature and respectful throughout the week, we would do a séance, a calling of past Camp Hollis spirits." To set the mood for a communication with the other side, Shaun, Foster and a few other counselors took the boys on a hike through the woods to look for the spot where, according to legend, former campers had died a tragic death. For some added drama, a counselor hidden in the woods provided sound effects. After a good scare, the group headed back to the Nature Cabin, where Foster and Shaun informed the campers that they were going to "call on the spirits of those campers." Shaun described the scene:

> Foster had prepared a series of strings attached to different objects throughout the cabin, and as spirits were called upon to make their presence known, objects would move: a chair slowly scratching across the floor, a tapping windowpane, a book falling to the floor and, for a bit of comedic relief (the campers were getting a little spooked at this point), a flushing toilet.

It wasn't just campers who were scared. Even the creative minds behind the séance couldn't explain it all. "When a random gust of wind came at the opportune time," Shaun admitted, "it even spooked Foster and me." Afterward, the lights came up, and Shaun, Foster and the helpers revealed their tricks to the campers. There were lots of questions and nobody slept really soundly that night, but it made for some memorable fun.

Tom Roshau might have the 2009 staff's séance beat with his 1980-era scary tale. Tom's story also started with a night hike for campers, led by him and his cabin co-counselor Ron Eldred (1985–87). But instead of children getting spooked, it was Tom who had to face his fears when he found himself face to face with El Diablo. Here's how Tom begins his legendary story:

> The summer of 1987 had been exceptionally rainy and our night hike destination was a swampy area far back in the misty forest. We groped our way through the midnight woods until finally the ground began to ooze over the tops of our sneakers. We had found The Swamp.
>
> As if on cue, the mist became thicker and the sounds of the night closed in around us. Frogs. Crickets. Something above quietly moving through

the trees. The campers became absolutely still. Someone (probably Ron) decided we should capture a frog as proof that we had reached The Swamp. Naturally, the campers all agreed with him, and since I wore the tallest boots, I was elected to capture the proof.

Whispers from Cabin 10 nudged me forward as I waded into the depths of The Swamp, my tall boots immediately surrendering to the taller swamp water. By now, I was literally knee-deep in the hunt, moving closer to a suspicious-looking gap in the reeds. I leaned in close, moved past the shadows. And froze.

The thing staring back at me seemed impossible. At one point in time, this monster may have indeed been classified as a frog, but that point was long past. I caught my breath and took a step back. Yes, I took a step back from a frog! As I inched farther away from it, the Frog-thing slowly hunched toward me. It assessed me…and dismissed me, turning his back as though I wasn't worth the effort. In truth, we both knew I wasn't.

Off balance, I splashed, lunged and fell to the safety of shore, to the back slaps and "better-luck-next-times" offered by Cabin 10. Because of the darkness, the campers hadn't seen the demon among the reeds; they merely thought I had tried for my target and missed. Wasting little time, I quickly rushed Cabin 10 back to camp, where I couldn't help but tell the story to my fellow counselors.

As Tom shared his story, it was embellished, and a group decided to go back, find the amphibious beast and conquer it. Tom would lead the way:

The gathering crowd enjoyed playing the role of the angry villagers, where talk of pitchforks and torches escalated until I suddenly realized I was being pushed back down the same trail I had sworn never to return. With the determined mob at my back, we finally arrived at a fork in the road. The path to the right led to the waiting arms of the Frog-thing. And the path to the left? I never hesitated. I took the path to the left.

With the rains we had seen that summer, I knew a safer "substitute swamp" would eventually appear somewhere to the left. But more importantly, we would be in the opposite direction of the Frog-thing. When that second swamp did come along, the villagers and I set up a perimeter where we watched and waited until the early hours of daybreak. In the end, we found nothing, because there was nothing ever there. The Devil in the Dark waited on the path to the right and I had taken the path to the left. Until this writing, no one has ever known the difference.

Although Tom and his group came back empty-handed, the story of their adventure did not die. Eventually, one of the counselors gave the Frog-thing a name, El Diablo. Soon, it became an official campfire story and, later, a song, with haunting lyrics like "Shut your windows, lock your doors, pull the covers tight. Don't go out on El Diablo night."

"That's odd. Snow in the middle of July?"

Three decades later, Tom's son Marshall, now a counselor himself, told his dad that Camp Hollis still held vigils for El Diablo. Even today, when children can stare at all sorts of frightening images on computer screens, groups of wide-eyed campers still sit at the edge of a midnight swamp, waiting for the Frog-thing to reveal itself. Each year, of course, nothing happens, because those campers are led on the wrong trail. Tom has no regrets:

> *I had met the Frog-thing face to face, I had lived to tell of it, and somewhere deep down I knew that kind of luck doesn't happen a second time around. I never regretted taking my friends to the left, so many summers ago. On that particular night in 1987, El Diablo was real.*

Scary night hikes on Lewis's Bluff have been around since Judge Sullivan founded Camp Hollis. It was early in the camp's history when children were first warned about a certain ghost that lives in the surrounding woods. Sightings of the spirit were initially reported by Judge Sullivan's son Mike and a co-counselor, who were leading an all-camp hike. On the walk, Mike explained, they found evidence of a man named George…George Hollis:

> *We used to take a five-mile hike with the kids to tire them out before bed. After walking quite a while, we'd find a place to build a campfire and roast hot dogs. Then we'd walk down Snake Swamp Road, which used to be quite scary for the kids. That's where the George Hollis story was born. John Kessler [1952–55], a fellow counselor, and I started talking about the swamp and he said something about a frog being squashed. "Do you think George Hollis did it?" he asked, and from there the legend of George Hollis, who rises out of the swamp to get children who are bad, was born.*

Camp Director Pat Sullivan (*left*) leads one of Hollis's many hikes, where stories like the "Legend of George Hollis" were born. *Courtesy of the Sullivan family.*

The story was scary enough to be a big hit with campers, and counselors elaborated on the story with each telling. Soon, the staff was coming up with situations where George could make an appearance, including at a Hollis Hop. Mike described one such Hop:

> *We dressed Kessler up with sheets and put him in the rafters above the dining hall. During the dance I yelled "Uh oh. I think George Hollis is here!" The kids got really scared. Now Dad loved the idea of the Hollis Hops and he attended them whenever he could, but when he saw the George Hollis antics, he wasn't too happy. He never wanted the children to be too frightened.*

Hollis counselors almost always obeyed Judge Sullivan's concerns for children, but the George Hollis story was just too much fun to forgo. And it wasn't just the guy counselors stirring up scary storylines. Kathy Klein (1957–59) also spent time up in those rafters—this time in the girls' dorm. From her lofty perch, she dropped pieces of lake seaweed while making ghost noises, bringing the spirit of George Hollis to life. For some campers, their fear was great fun. Camper Christine Fisher described it as "the marvelous thrill of terror."

George Hollis was reborn each summer, thanks to a new group of creative counselors. By the late 1950s, George's backstory had expanded. Cindy Czerow Nacey remembered his legend like this: "He lived nearby and had a dog that he walked around camp. One night he walked into the swamp and got lost and never came back." A decade later, the plight of George Hollis had been turned into a full-length story, complete with a moral. Since then, campers hear it at the first campfire of each session:

> *Many years ago, when Camp Hollis first began, George Hollis was known as the best counselor. Highly respected by the other staff and loved by children, George was in charge of explaining the rules to each new group of campers. There were obvious rules: no running unless you're in a sports game, make your beds every morning, brush your teeth twice a day. But the most important rule, which George saved for last, was to never go in the woods alone. This was important, George told the campers, because there was a patch of quicksand just off one of the trails. Several unlucky children had been sucked into it and died.*
>
> *George made sure that one camper in particular, Jimmy Gimme, was listening. Jimmy was an unruly child and not about to listen to counselors. So one night, while the rest of the camp was sleeping, Jimmy left his bed, snuck out of the building and headed straight toward the woods. When his counselor counted the number of sleeping heads he noticed one was missing—Jimmy Gimme! The staff, well aware of Jimmy's antics, knew he'd headed off to the woods. In the dead of night, most counselors were afraid to begin the search, but George volunteered. Holding his trusty flashlight and wearing his favorite baseball cap, he headed off into the dark, alone.*
>
> *As dawn broke, Jimmy came running to the camp, screaming that George was trapped in the quicksand. He explained that he himself had fallen into the thick muck and when George heard the boy's screams, the heroic counselor reached for a branch above the quicksand and pulled Jimmy out. Then the branch snapped and George fell in, immediately starting to sink.*
>
> *With their leader in danger, several counselors headed off to rescue him, returning with only his cap found floating on the quicksand. The grief-stricken staff buried the cap behind the Arts & Crafts building and placed a huge rock atop it.*

Counselors promise each new group of campers that, in the morning, they'll take a walk to see that rock, which seems like a good ending for a ghost story. But there's more. As children huddle around the campfire, feeling the

darkness set in on their first night at Camp Hollis, they hear the counselors warn, in one unified voice: NEVER GO INTO THE WOODS ALONE!

For decades, there was a second, equally scary, reason not to enter the Camp Hollis woods unescorted. Found on the trails, not far from the quicksand site, was an abandoned bus. Nothing in the camp's recorded history explains when the bus first appeared or how it managed to maneuver through trees and thick brush to park itself near the Hollis campgrounds. But facts don't really matter when it comes to storytelling. As campers stood at the bus, staring at the mysterious rusted heap, counselors wove believable and unbelievable legends: It was a makeshift home for a hobo who terrorized children. It had once carried boys and girls to the first day of Camp Hollis but was ambushed by wild woods people. The bus had magic powers, and if you got too close, it could suck you inside, just like the nearby quicksand. Tales told of the bus were as creative as the counselors who thought them up.

Ghost stories are not everyone's cup of tea. There are adults who will tell you they never went back for a second summer of Camp Hollis because of the frightening stories that took up residence in their young minds. Thankfully, camp directors and counselors introduced other traditions for children to remember, and in the mid-1990s, they came up with a real gem: something called Candlelight.

Camp Hollis has Forrest LaBarre to thank for Candlelight. Forrest had been a Hollis counselor and assistant director during his 1980s summers at the camp. In 1996, now living in Oregon, he contacted the Youth Bureau, looking to return to the camp as director while he and his wife were visiting the East Coast. Forrest's career was centered on youth and recreation, and when he showed up ready to lead the Hollis staff, he brought some innovative ideas, including Candlelight.

Picture this scene: It's the last night of a camp session, and everyone gathers for a ceremony—the stage in the woods, the fire circle or, if the waters are calm, on the lakeshore. As every camper and staff person takes their place, they are handed a small votive candle. Counselors take turns reminiscing about the week at camp, and then children are invited to reflect on what it meant to be a Hollis camper. Sometimes soft music plays; other times crickets and frogs provide the soundtrack. One by one, candles are lit, their tiny flame passed from person to person.

As with all activities and traditions at Camp Hollis, the staff is responsible for Candlelight. Aware that the ceremony is the last major event for each group of campers, counselors strive to create something memorable. Jeff Von Wald's 1997 Candlelight included a reference to the book *The Little Prince*, the beloved story of a boy who learns about friendship with a fox and a rose. Jeff and other staff had shared the book at a campfire earlier in the week, and he mentioned it during Candlelight:

> *Our time here is on the verge of ending and I'm going to ask you to think back to your very first moments at camp. Perhaps this place meant little to you, like the Prince to the fox. The people around you were like thousands*

In recent years, children say goodbye to their Camp Hollis experience with a special ceremony known as Candlelight. *Courtesy of the Camp Hollis Archives.*

"Our daughter says she can't fall asleep until we do something called Candlelight."

you had seen before, like the bunches of roses were to the Prince. You may have felt excited or you may have felt homesick or nervous. You sought friends like the Little Prince sought a friend and his special rose, and you didn't find them here right away. You were like the Little Prince, far away from home…

Now think how you feel about camp as we sit here together tonight. Think about what or who it is that made those changes in feelings happen. As we have seen the setting of the sun and we look into the twilight of our time together, these people who meant little to you at the beginning are now unique because you have invested your time in them and they in you. Together we have laughed, we have cried. Was it all just to toss behind us and leave? Did the Little Prince think his beloved rose was to leave behind? Or could it be that every one of our experiences at camp are the rain and soil that have made us into each other's rose?

When Jeff ended his talk by saying, "You have people here who care about you. This is your home as well," it wasn't just children who understood the profound experience of Camp Hollis. Counselors felt it, too, especially in the final days of August, as they prepared to leave their summer home, their summer family and those unforgettable Camp Hollis traditions. As staff person Ali Martin described it, "I don't think I've ever been so continuously emotionally moved as I was every Thursday night for our Candlelight ceremonies."

STAYING STRONG
WITH GOOD FRIENDS

How has Camp Hollis been able to offer its full days of activities and long-standing traditions year after year? Why is it still a vital youth program despite a radical shift in how children spend their recreational and leisure time? And, perhaps most importantly, how has the County of Oswego managed to support the camp through tough financial times, continuing its pledge to provide for the well-being of children? The answer to those questions—the solution to every camp challenge, if you will—grew from a philosophy that both Dr. Hollis and Judge Sullivan adopted early in the camp's development.

Both of the camp's founders were known for creating strong partnerships with other youth-serving organizations. In Dr. Hollis's case, it was medical professionals, hospitals and charitable organizations. For Sullivan, it was his work with orphanages, schools, social service agencies and law enforcement. If a group had a child's best interest in mind, Sullivan in particular found a way to collaborate with them. A fine example of this came in the 1950s, when he added the 4-H program to his list of Camp Hollis friends.

Sponsored by the Oswego County's chapter of Cornell Cooperative Extension, 4-H's mission mirrored Sullivan's goals for children. It was stated clearly in its name, its 4 "H"s promising "my head to clearer thinking, my heart to greater loyalty, my hands to larger service, and my health to better living, for my club, my community, my country, and my world." Youngsters had been reciting that pledge since 1902, when 4-H was founded in Ohio. New York State followed suit in 1925, in Suffolk County. That same year, Oswego County, with its strong ties to 4-H's agricultural focus, hosted its first clubs in rural farm communities. By the time Camp Hollis opened, Judge Sullivan had befriended the county's Cooperative Extension director, Bill Cheney, and in 1952, he extended an offer to Cheney: bring your youngsters to Hollis for a camporee.

Cheney accepted the offer but bargained for more than one campout. He and Sullivan agreed to fit a 4-H weekend program in between each of Hollis's four camp sessions. Barbara Mandigo was the development coordinator for 4-H Oswego County and was there when Cheney accepted Sullivan's offer. With her long tenure with 4-H Camp Hollis—she was assistant director from 1953 to 1958 and then director from 1959 until she retired in 1975—Barbara collected many Hollis memories:

> *We were there two days and one night. We brought in our own staff and held two training schools for them before camp started. The county provided bedding, towels, laundry, food and a doctor for exams at the start of camp at Saturday noon. After a few years, we charged each camper two dollars a weekend to help pay for the cook and lifeguards.*
>
> *Campers were divided into four groups, with two classes held Saturday afternoon and two on Sunday afternoon. The classes were usually nature study, first aid, sports and crafts. Professor John Weeks, from the college, helped train our counselors and often came to camp on Saturdays to take the campers on nature hikes. Sunday morning we had worship service in camp.*

Sharon Figiera was one of the 4-H children enjoying Hollis camporees. She'd joined her Hannibal 4-H Club in 1955, and the following year, ten-year-old Sharon headed off to Hollis with her fellow club members:

> *Camp Hollis seemed like a long trip from Hannibal, but we quickly enjoyed the many activities offered in the fresh air: walking in the woods, learning about nature, and playing baseball, football, dodgeball and the ever-loved tetherball. On hot days, walking across the stony beach was well worth the refreshing cool, or sometimes cold, swim in the lake. Some nights there was campfire on the bluff; other nights they held dances, with a favorite being square dancing.*
>
> *For several years, our club's members continued going to camp, making new friends from around the county. At the time, there were 4-H county events like dress reviews, which judged our sewing projects, and demonstration days, where we showed how we'd learned to cook a meal or other such projects. We often met our Camp Hollis friends at those events.*

For most 4-Hers, Hollis camporees ended when they aged out of the program. But not for Sharon:

> *I graduated from 4-H camper to counselor when I was 14. We still participated in all the activities, but also made sure campers were safe. We were expected to help in the kitchen, set tables, serve food, clean up and do dishes by hand. I don't remember getting paid; having fun was enough.*

Occasionally, a 4-H counselor joined the regular Camp Hollis staff, and in 1976, Sarah Gould Hill did double duty, working both camps back to back. "It was my summer with no vacation," Sarah remembered. "I'd get home after finishing a week of Camp Hollis, do a load of laundry, and head right back for another 4-H Hollis weekend."

Camp Hollis and Cooperative Extension continued its joint 4-H weekend camp program until 1997, but the two organizations' long-standing pledge to serve youth did not end. There were innovative 4-H projects at Hollis that challenged club members, including one involving their clothing and textile program. County clubs were asked to create new curtains for the camp's cabin windows, and one autumn day in 1993, several club members showed up at Hollis with yardsticks and a notepad. After jotting down window sizes and brainstorming kid-friendly patterns, the youngsters headed back to their hometowns, where they turned eighty-five yards of fabric into fifty-seven curtains.

Measuring was critical to another Cooperative Extension/Camp Hollis collaboration, but the 4-Hers involved in this one needed more sophisticated equipment than a yardstick. Throughout its history, Camp Hollis has developed a number of trails in its thirty acres of woods, and by the 1990s, those half dozen pathways took visitors to a pond, a stream and several lookout points along the bluff. While no one was ever going to get hopelessly lost in the Hollis forest—its borders are Lake Ontario, the widely known Nunzi's property and a country road—navigating it could still be intimidating to first-time hikers. A trail map could help.

To create Hollis's first comprehensive property map, camp officials reached out to Steve Brown, an Oswego County Cooperative Extension natural resources agent, and in 1996, Steve guided a group of 4-Hers through the steps of creating an accurate trail map, using a brand-new technology known as Global Positioning Systems (GPS). As Steve recalled, he had no idea that creating the map with those youngsters was groundbreaking:

I'm pretty certain Camp Hollis was the first summer camp in the nation that used Geographic Information Systems and GPS to have its boundaries, trails and features mapped by young people. By today's standards, the equipment we had barely worked, and it was extremely complicated and expensive. There were so few GPS satellites in orbit back then that we would walk a short distance and have to wait for the system to collect our data and "catch up."

Today, with cellphones' GPS providing maps in an instant, it's hard to imagine an electronic device operating as slow as Steve's did. But he noticed how much his 4-Hers enjoyed connecting their trail exploration to an orbiting satellite. They talked about their mapping activity with friends back home, and it wasn't long before more sophisticated GPS devices had those kids back outside enjoying an activity known as geocaching. Today, millions of the young and young-at-heart head out into nature, using their phones to lead them to hidden treasures. Thanks to its partnership with 4-H, Camp Hollis was one step ahead of everyone else.

While Hollis is fortunate to have its facility maintained by Oswego County's Building & Grounds and DPW crews, those busy departments haven't always been able to work on smaller camp improvement projects. To tackle those, camp administrators often rely on the Boy and Girl Scouts, which offer youth an Eagle Scout or Gold Award for completing projects, like new seating at the fire circle or an update to the ballfield. And when it comes to trail maintenance, Camp Hollis relies on a team of teenagers sponsored by a federally funded work study program. When it was founded in the 1970s, the Comprehensive Employment and Training Act (CETA) chose Camp Hollis as one of its first worksites.[*]

These work study programs are run by Oswego County's Department of Employment and Training, and its Summer Youth Employment Program has given lots of young people their first job. Bill Boyea (1985–87) is well aware of CETA's accomplishments at Camp Hollis. Bill watched a crew work on trails when he was a camper in 1976 and then led activities on those upgraded trails as a Hollis counselor. After graduating from SUNY's College of Environmental Science and Forestry, Bill spent three years as a Summer Youth Employment Program crew supervisor. Along with clearing dead trees and trimming brush from the trails, he and his crew created some Hollis attractions:

---

[*] In later years, CETA was replaced by the Job Training Partnership Act (JTPA) and then by the Workforce Investment Act (WIA).

Since I'd worked as a counselor, I knew there was a small open area in the woods with some primitive log seating where we'd take our campers to perform various spur-of-the-moment skits or take in the sounds of nature. Our crew proposed turning it into a performance area with a wooden stage and improved seating. Except for the planks, the material for the stage and seating came from the woods.

I'd often taken my campers on a hike to the pond when I was a counselor. There was a trail around it and I thought a deck would give children a better observation point. I planned it out on paper and showed it to Camp Director Judy McManus. When I became crew leader, I got to carry out those plans. Like our work on the stage, most of the material to frame the deck came from trees in the woods.

Improvements to the camp's trails continued, and beginning in the spring of 1992, Camp Hollis was fortunate to have Dave Warner lead a crew in that work. Dave came to the camp with ten years of experience supervising youth conservation crews, and he had a keen eye for how to best improve a nature facility for children. When Dave reflected on his five seasons at Camp Hollis, he explained why he and his crew chose their first project:

The camp wanted to offer visitors an opportunity to explore the wooded area in all seasons, but in the spring or after heavy rains those trails were like mud pits. The County Highway Department delivered mountains of gravel to a spot at the beginning of the trails. Since the trails were so marshy and narrow, our crew had to move those gravel mountains one wheelbarrow at a time.

Estimates of the total trail Dave and his crew covered, wheelbarrow by wheelbarrow, is about three miles, and it took them nearly that whole first summer. But what a difference it made. Even today, nearly thirty years after that hard labor, the trails are navigable year-round.

Now that they were on more solid ground, Dave and his crew racked up an impressive list of trail projects. They built an observation tower at the highest point of the camp's bluff. ("We wanted to give people a greater vista of the Great Lake," Dave explained.) They moved the amphitheater stage to a more hospitable location. ("We used shaved logs to roll the stage, all in one piece, on the trails.") Dave taught his young crew how to make the pond more interesting. ("A log chained to a weight was set in the middle of the pond and campers loved seeing turtles on top of it, sunning themselves.") He designed and built a challenge course off one of the trails, moving team building and interpersonal activities into the outdoors. ("Camp Hollis and Youth Bureau staff had gone on a retreat, where we worked together on a ropes course. We used some of those ideas to re-create the experience at Hollis.")

All of Dave Warner's trail projects continue to serve the camp, including one that visitors can appreciate without even going for a nature walk. It's a trailhead that welcomes hikers into the Hollis forest. The all-wood structure, which arches above the beginning of the main trail, was created from some cut saplings. Dave and his crew first immersed them in pond water to increase their pliability and then curved them to look like the rays of a Camp Hollis sunset.

I asked Dave how he was able to construct such durable camp improvements with an unskilled crew of teenagers. He offered this key to their success: "I sat down with the crew before each project and explained what the camp needed. Then I asked their opinions on how each project should look and how we could best tackle it. What the crew decided didn't always look exactly like I'd envisioned, but what we created for the camp, we created together."

Crew leader Dave Warner (*far right*) guided youth workers through a variety of Camp Hollis nature and outdoor improvements. *Courtesy of the Oswego County Office of Promotion & Tourism.*

Another of Hollis's long-lasting partnerships has been with Oswego County schools. Along with future teachers from the Oswego College working summers at the camp and school administrators serving on its advisory board, Hollis has long been a field trip destination for school groups. Many high school students celebrated their graduation at the camp, watching the sun set on one part of their life as a new one begins. But the strongest camp-school ties are those with the teachers who have considered Camp Hollis an ideal setting for students to work on their three "R"s. For more than thirty years, that's what the fourth-grade teaching staff at Hannibal Central School has done. Each September, five or six classrooms of fourth graders and their adult chaperones head to the camp for two full days of outdoor education instruction. Hannibal teacher Mary Lee O'Brien, one of the program's founders, explained their goal:

The field trip to Camp Hollis builds trust and community across our classrooms. Our motto was "We Sink or Swim Together." Students were responsible for keeping their cabins clean, and were assigned duties in the main lodge and kitchen areas. Parents were involved in the preparation and serving of food. We partnered with SUNY Oswego students and professors, offering education majors an opportunity to gain experience while helping us provide a fulfilling, safe experience for all.

Proof of Hannibal's school-to-camp success can be found in journals the fourth graders kept during their trip. When student Brandon Miano went to Hollis, in October 2009, his journal captured every memory, beginning with safety tips: "We joined Matt Wood [2005–6, 2017–18], the Challenge Course Ropes leader, and he told us to be careful of where the poison ivy was. Then we went to the swinging log, which we had to walk across. Matt told us that if we needed help, we would just have to say 'Help.'"

As would be expected, Brandon and his fellow students spent most of their two-day stay outdoors, where he experienced journal-worthy events like the science-based nature walk. ("We went right in the woods to watch how nature works in real life, how trees work by giving oxygen.") He learned to see geometry in the world. ("We had to find some shapes like spheres and spirals and then we went to the Arts & Crafts building to make a picture of what we'd found.") Brandon and his classmates filled up buckets with pond water, where, as his teachers instructed, his "learning looks" would help him use a hand lens to observe frogs, fish, weeds and "some little bugs and a red worm we found." Heading down to the beach,

Brandon's teachers provided a unique geology lesson. ("We put some rice and sugar in a bag and shook it up. We saw what was on top and what was on bottom.") Pointing to the bluff, the teachers then asked students to look for similar signs of how the earth had settled.

Seeing the world in real time, not from a textbook, has had a lasting effect on Hannibal fourth graders. When those students prepare to graduate from high school, they're asked to name the highlight of their school career. Many mention their Camp Hollis field trip. And as Mary Lee O'Brien expressed, "The fact that the educators at Hannibal continue to plan and carry out this experience is testimony to the positive impact it has on everyone who was lucky enough to be part of it."

Over in the Central Square School District, Frances Knighton would agree. For many years, she and her second, third and fourth graders traveled from Cleveland Elementary School to Hollis for a three-day/two-night adventure. Frances always prepared a thick booklet of what students and parent chaperones needed to know in order for their field trip to succeed. It was a textbook of sorts, ranging from tips on how to identify wildlife to the steps of making a s'more. Along with those gems of knowledge, Mrs. Knighton's rules were clearly stated. Everyone was expected to participate in meal prep and cabin cleanup, which included a shift of emptying garbage cans and running a vacuum cleaner.

It was holistic education at its best, as Cleveland Elementary student Cody Netzband reported in his June 1999 trip journal. Cody logged important lessons on nutrition ("Our menu was subs, chips, and fruit—we could pick from apples, bananas, oranges or grapes"), environmental science ("My dad and I collected rocks, shells and driftwood") and meteorology ("From the top of the observation tower we had a great view of the lake"). The camp was an ideal spot for physical education too. ("I learned how to dive at the pool and hit a homerun on the ballfield that went halfway to the basketball court!") Cody ended his journal by saying, "I like Camp Hollis a lot and that's why I want to go again."

Cody *did* end up back at Hollis, but not as a student. In the summers of 2011, '12 and '13, while earning his education degree, Cody joined the Camp Hollis summer staff, first working as an activity leader and then as co-director. In his student journal, written a dozen years before he would end up helping to run Camp Hollis, Cody filled blank pages with samples of leaves and ferns and drawings of animals seen on the trails. But they were more than memories for a little boy—they were reminders of what was waiting for him when he returned to Camp Hollis.

One school-based program making its annual field trip to Hollis didn't come for a day or an overnight, but for a full six weeks. With their lengthy stay, the Oswego County BOCES Deaf Education students were learning plenty, but so were the campers and counselors who welcomed them. Those collaborative educational opportunities began in 1986, when BOCES teacher Nancy Cooper took a summer job as an interpreter for the deaf at Camp Iroquois, a day program in Manlius, New York. BOCES's Deaf Education program provides learning for its children year-round, and some of Nancy's students attended Camp Iroquois as a summer school experience. As she observed their enthusiastic participation at the camp, she got an idea.

"I told my supervisor, Sandy Van Shaack, about the good experience our students had at Camp Iroquois," Nancy said. "One of the great things about Sandy is you could bring her an idea and she would make it happen." Van Shaack, who was BOCES's assistant director of special education, went to work on Nancy's idea: a summer school program at a camp closer to Oswego County schools.

"In order for our program to qualify as a summer school," Sandy explained, "it had to continue their school year environment. That meant a setting where deaf and hard of hearing children would integrate with hearing children. When we began looking for such a setting, we thought of Camp Hollis and hoped that Oswego County officials would consider hosting our program."

Sandy contacted Oswego City-County Youth Bureau director Kathy Fenlon, who discussed it with the camp's supervisor, Dave Canfield. After a few brainstorming sessions with the BOCES staff, Camp Hollis welcomed the school-camp merger. To test their idea, in the summer of 1988, Nancy and co-teacher Tammy Seymour brought their students to Camp Hollis on Fridays. "We had lunch there and joined in a few activities," Nancy recalled. The program worked so well that, in 1989, Camp Hollis became a six-week school day program for BOCES.

The program's first hurdle to overcome was where to hold classes at a camp that takes place almost exclusively outdoors. It wasn't much, but Hollis offered a small section of the Arts & Crafts building that was being used as a maintenance storage area. In 1990, BOCES teacher Kathy Titman set up her classroom there. "I had a small shelf for my school supplies among the hammers, saws and other equipment," Kathy remembered. "It was tight quarters, but the camp staff welcomed us."

BOCES teachers saw results as soon as their students began splitting the school day between academics and integration into camp activities.

"Because our students came from all over Oswego County, they were often the only deaf person in their school," Nancy said. "At Hollis, they found a peer group. Kids who wouldn't say two words in their home schools were signing conversations at camp. We think it was because of the camp's relaxed atmosphere."

"Our students also got a chance to gain confidence in their social skills," Kathy explained. "This happened because Hollis staff welcomed our students. Our kids gave each counselor a sign language name by combining a staff person's job or hobby with the first letter of their name. For example, the camp nurse Dorothy's sign was the letter *D* placed on the signer's wrist, as if he or she was taking a pulse."

Over the years, the BOCES teachers and students found meaningful ways to further integrate into the Hollis program. The group organized an annual overnight camping experience, stretching the school day to include teachable moments such as working as a team to pitch a tent. It was a first time away from home for many children, who got to watch the sun set over the lake and attend a campfire. "Some of our students had never had a s'more before," Nancy said.

Thanks to their BOCES friends, Hollis staff and campers got to try new things too. Learning took place at lunchtime, when a school student would start each meal by teaching a new sign or sharing something about the deaf culture, such as how hearing aids work. Nature director Jim Hooper got a big lesson in inclusion by working with Deaf Education students:

> *In the Nature game "Bat and Moth" we gather in a circle. In the middle, a blindfolded camper (the Bat) tries to tag a sighted camper (the Moth). When one of the kids from BOCES said that he wanted to be the Bat, I thought, "He's already deaf and now he's going to be blind. How is this going to work?" It was an awkward moment, but his teacher said, "Go ahead and let him try." So I blindfolded the student and after a while he did find the Moth. I asked him how he was able to without verbal cues. "I sat on the ground," he said, "and felt where the vibrations were coming from and went in that direction." It was a real eye-opener for me: When you lose one sense, the others become heightened.*

It's been thirty-two years since the BOCES Summer School program began (today BOCES is known as the Center for Instruction, Technology & Innovation, or CiTi), and the students it serves at Camp Hollis have diversified. "With medical advancements, we now know that hearing loss can be attributed to many different factors," Kathy explained. "Today we have children who are on the autism spectrum or who have hearing but are nonverbal. What hasn't changed is how our students thrive here. I call it the magic of Camp Hollis."

Kathy shared an example of the magic she's witnessed many times in her three decades with the program. Her story involves two students, Tonaya and Robert. Robert, a ten-year-old boy with autism, is nonverbal and wears hearing aids. He was having a hard time expressing his wants and needs, and as Kathy noted,

due to sensory issues, Robert often had outbursts that could become physical...not from anger, but from lack of language and too much sensory input. He required a lot of adult supervision. One morning, while everyone was putting on their equipment, I watched tiny Tonaya, age five, approach Robert with his hearing aid in her hand. She spoke without words, just eye contact and an innocent spirit that said, "Let me help you." Robert slowly angled his head and offered his ear to her. Together they put in his hearing aids.

Nearly all of Camp Hollis's partnerships have centered on creating healthy recreation and education programs for children, but in the 1990s, camp administrators expanded their definition of youth to include the young at heart. They called their new program Senior Camping, and no, Hollis wasn't targeting high school seniors—it was welcoming those students' grandparents.

The new program began when Judy Talbot, a recreation specialist for the Oswego County town of Scriba, learned about a successful camp for seniors in the Rochester area. Judy visited the program and shared the enthusiasm she witnessed there with the Oswego City-County Youth Bureau, suggesting that Scriba and the county partner in a similar program. Other agencies, like the Office for the Aging and the Retired Senior Volunteer Program (RSVP), joined in, and in the fall of 1992, the camp held a day-only program of crafts, nature walks and a sandwich lunch. As the organizers were thanking everyone for attending, one woman stood up and declared, "This was fun, but we wanna stay overnight!"

By the next year, a new type of camper was showing up at Hollis with a suitcase and sleeping bag, excited for an overnight party. There were two full days of programs: endless Arts & Crafts sessions, up close and personal introductions to hobbies like beekeeping and raising alpacas, tips on how

Twice a year, the young at heart enjoy their fun in the sun at Camp Hollis's Senior Camping program. *Courtesy of the Camp Hollis Archives.*

to keep a canoe from tipping and the joyful experience of pulling a bow string and sending an arrow straight to the bull's-eye. Word spread, and soon Senior Camping was at capacity, with attendees arriving early to claim their favorite bunk.

After several years of the campout being organized by agency personnel, those enjoying the program offered to take the lead. It made sense. Seniors know best what they consider fun, and soon a dedicated group of Senior Campers were making the decisions. Here's how Sandy Davis, who's coordinated the event for many years, explained the opening day of each busy campout:

> *It's up in the morning at 5:35 and off to Camp Hollis. By 7:00 am, committee member Pat shows up with four boxes of fruits and vegetables from Ontario Orchards. Roberta brings in our garage sale and auction "stuff." Peggy and Fran sort T-shirts and items for our camp store. Other committee members cut up fruits and quarter donuts from Dunkin'. I make coffee and hot water; Kim makes orange drink from McDonalds and sorts through donated vegetables to create our dinner menu. Imo mans the till, registering the arrivals. We make it a happy day for all.*

Happiness comes in all varieties at Senior Camping. For Joanne Harter, who enjoys just about every aspect of the camp but especially loves the rocky shoreline, "I could stay there for hours, whether with my sister [Joanne attends with her twin, Suzanne Brown], my camping sisters or by myself. The expanse of rounded stones is what draws me—so alike, but each a distinct individual."

Many first-timers at Senior Camping find their stay pleasurable, but there's a special joy for those returning to the camp after decades. For them, the memories they make now rekindle those from their youth. Here's how Susan Talamo Kubis explained it after her first Senior Camping visit:

> *My most awesome summer memories as a child were at Camp Hollis. My Dad felt the camp was the best deal he got from his county taxes and I went year after year. In 1958, we "fibbed" about my age so I could go a year early, and in 1961, we "fibbed" again so I could attend an extra year.... Today, 50+ years later, I'm having another great time at Camp Hollis. The lake is just as clear and beautiful as I remember. And there will be a full moon tonight. Perfect, because Camp Hollis still has that magical feel.*

Daphne Thompson, a Senior Camping regular, felt that same magic and expressed it in a poem, which included these stanzas:

> *Camp Hollis is the place to go,*
> *when one is feeling very low.*
> *It cheers the mind and spirit, too,*
> *as the waters we doth view.*
>
> *Splendid is the atmosphere,*
> *as we bring each other cheer.*
> *Fellowship is one glad thing*
> *that the seniors have to bring.*
>
> *The sun comes out, so hot and bright,*
> *it makes for a very blissful night.*
> *Delightment in the setting sun*
> *we watch the beauty 'til it's done...*

Until it's done. In the years I was involved with the Senior Camping program, that's the greatest lesson I learned. With each gathering, I'd notice some longtime regular campers were missing, denied another campout due to declining health or their untimely passing. That's when a phrase I'd heard seniors offer to one another started to make sense. As they pack their cars to head home, hugs are given, along with this goodbye: "See you next year, God willing."

Learning to accept the inevitability of death is the main focus of another program Camp Hollis created with a partnering agency. In 2000, the Youth Bureau was contacted by Oswego County's Hospice Services Department, which provides support for families of those with a terminal illness. The hospice staff was exploring ways to offer respite to the family members who are perhaps least equipped to handle the death of a loved one: children. Hospice's idea was to create a supportive environment in a relaxed setting—a children's camp would be perfect—where girls and boys could begin to acknowledge and accept their grief. They called their idea Camp Rainbow of Hope.

By August 2001, Donna Hopkins, an Oswego County Hospice nurse, had teamed up with Camp Hollis staff and the Friends of Oswego County Hospice to institute the three-day/two-night program. Donna took responsibility for lining up trained bereavement counselors and workshop leaders, while Hollis personnel designed a daily schedule for traditional camp fun. Friends of Oswego County Hospice provided funding for food and supplies. Interspersed with swimming, sports and crafts, Donna designed several "healing circles," small group gatherings where children could talk about their loss in a safe setting. Some of those children were as young as six, and to help them understand how to express grief, Donna recruited a group of volunteers called "big buddies": teenagers who would role model how to share emotions.

The big buddy program became a key factor in Rainbow of Hope's success. The teens were old enough to help lead the discussions yet young enough for the campers to identify with. And as can be expected, being at camp became as transformational for the soon-to-be adults as it was for the children. Here are two big buddy stories.

Kyle Thompson was ten years old when his father died in a motorcycle accident. Two years later, he and his brother and sister were invited to attend Camp Rainbow in its inaugural year. Kyle described the camp as "awesome. [I was] finally able to talk about what I had been through with kids my own age who had been through the same things I had. The healing circles were great. We did activities that helped with the grieving process and helped kids open up."

Kyle really benefited and enjoyed his summer at Camp Rainbow, but there was a problem. As a twelve-year-old, he had aged out of the program as a camper but was too young to be a big buddy. Donna, however, saw the importance for the program's continuity and knew that some Rainbow campers, like Kyle, would eventually make great big buddies. She offered Kyle an option. "On the last day of camp, Donna asked if I would like to be what she affectionately called a 'guinea pig,' a trial test of having a camper come back to train as a big buddy."

Kyle enthusiastically accepted Donna's offer, and after two years of preparation, he moved into the big buddy role, returning each year until college obligations shortened his summer. In his many years at Camp Rainbow, Kyle moved up the ranks, eventually becoming a healing circle facilitator, where he sat with grieving children, offering the same comfort he'd once received. Looking back, Kyle thinks of Camp Rainbow of Hope as "one of the best things I have done with my life."

Erin Dowd's Rainbow experience was as powerful as Kyle's. Her mother, Michelle, was an Oswego County hospice nurse, and as she learned about the healing work going on at Camp Rainbow, Michelle thought of her teenage daughter. Perhaps Erin would consider devoting some of her summer to help the camp accomplish its goals? Erin agreed, but little did she know what Rainbow would mean to her, a sentiment she captured in a college essay:

> During the course of my relatively short life, few instances have been prominent as milestones of my maturity. Besides the routine graduations, birthdays and other symbolic traditions of growing up, I cannot recall many instances in which I realized that I have truly grown. Although my motives to participate in Camp Rainbow of Hope were not to develop my moral fiber and I did not expect to connect with the individuals I would meet, both were results of my three-day experience…
>
> At the camp, I came to the stark realization that the world is not a perfect place and it will never be. But that doesn't mean we can't be content with what we are given. These lively children showed me that there are times to be sad, times to play and be happy, and you should always ask for help and be willing to give help when it is needed. During those three days, I was lucky enough to experience the magnitude of forces we have no control over and the strength of the human spirit. I went to camp to give my hand to these children, but they left with my heart.

At the end of each Rainbow camp, the staff and children gather around a freshly dug hole. A young tree, its roots bound in a container, sits off to the side. Ceremonially, each person writes a short note to their deceased loved one and drops it in the hole. The sapling is then set in place, and one by one, each person tosses a shovelful of dirt around the tree's roots, covering the notes. A sprinkling from a watering can completes the activity. Today, walking the Camp Hollis property, one can see several of these thriving testimonies—beautiful reminders of how people coming together to grieve death can find a renewed purpose to live.

Camp Rainbow of Hope has received much praise for its service to grieving children. The program's organizers have heard from parents, guardians, schoolteachers and social workers who've noticed a change in youngsters after attending the camp. In 2002, an acknowledgement of Rainbow's work came from beyond Oswego County—far beyond. At a ceremony in Washington, D.C., the camp received the National Association of Counties' Volunteer of the Year award. Although it was a surprise for those who'd worked on the program, the award made sense. Months before the ceremony, on September 11, 2001, our country was attacked, and with that tragedy, Americans had to collectively accept and then begin healing their grief. In choosing Rainbow, the National Association acknowledged the lessons that can be learned at a camp founded on hope.

A second new partnership was created at Camp Hollis in 2001, this one looking to serve not only children in need but also their families. The request came from Rural & Migrant Ministries of Oswego County, a charitable service founded by three Catholic nuns who had been assigned to churches in the county's north country. The Ministries provides medical care, a food pantry and social services for impoverished families. While working with their clientele, one of the nuns, Sister Louise Machia, saw that these families never got a vacation from their troubled lives. Wanting to offer them some respite, Sister Machia asked Camp Hollis to partner with the Ministries: she would recruit families and procure food and supply donations, while Hollis staff provided recreation programs. Coming up with the program's name was easy. Machia called it Family Camp.

The four-day/three-night getaway was like a trip to an all-expenses-paid vacation for the Ministries' families. Each family unit (sometimes several generations attended together) was given a cabin as their home away from home. But unlike life back home, mothers did not have to prepare meals, wash clothes or keep children occupied. This was a new experience for the Ministries' families, just as it was for Camp Hollis staff, who watched the program take on a life of its own.

Staff planned to offer a traditional camp schedule, with families beginning each morning at the flagpole, followed by breakfast and a daylong roster of sports, crafts and swimming. There were to be hourly rotations so families could enjoy each activity together: moms and dads kicking a soccer ball with their kids and Grandma learning how to boondoggle with the youngsters. But that's not what happened. The adults attending Family Camp made it known that they preferred a more casual "drop in when you feel like it" program. Perfectly happy to set up a lounge chair outside their cabin, parents watched their children play as the sun rose, shined and set.

The camp schedule suffered its biggest "failure" with Hollis's proposed evening activities. Nature hikes and softball tournaments were planned, but campers young and old had something else in mind. The year that Family Camp began, its attendees, like our whole country, were captivated by a new television show, *American Idol*. In a case of life imitating art, members of the Ministries' families requested their own version of the talent show. So staff threw out their plans, and on the final night of Family Camp, the stage was set for *Camp Hollis Idol*.

"There they go again. Trading stories about their days at Camp Hollis."

A microphone was placed at one end of the dining hall. At the opposite end, rows of chairs were filled with an enthusiastic audience. One by one, singers, karate enthusiasts, aspiring comedians and storytellers were called to the stage. There were memorable performances: a boy with a severe speech impediment overcame his shyness to tell corny jokes; a young girl sang one Patsy Cline song after another, each one generating a louder round of applause; and a teenager had the entire camp in tears with his a cappella rendition of Randy Travis's "Three Wooden Crosses."

Sunday mornings, just before families packed up their Camp Hollis memories, the pastor from the nearby Newman Center church arrived with his guitar. If the day cooperated, the late August sun was still strong as the families' combined voices sent hymns of praise into blue skies. For some in attendance, it was a new experience: the feeling of having much to be thankful for.

Although Senior Camping and Family Camp were new ways that Hollis served Oswego County, they weren't the first time grownups got to experience the fun children kept talking about. As far back as 1975, the county decided there ought to be opportunities for everybody in the family to visit Camp Hollis. That year, Oswego County Legislators expanded how their recreational facility could be used, renaming it Camp Hollis Park. Along with summer weekends, when the children's camp was not in operation, organized youth groups, human services agencies and families were now able to book the camp in the spring, once the lake-effect snow finally melted, and the fall, before Old Man Winter again took control.

This shift in how and when the camp could be enjoyed introduced myriad new events at Hollis. Sports teams had an entire facility to work on skill-building. Social service departments held retreats, enjoying the beauty of nature while conducting workshops and brainstorming new programs. Families found the campgrounds to be an ideal setting for picnics, graduation celebrations, birthday parties and even weddings. Over the years, a few families have learned that a getaway at Camp Hollis is a great way to maintain close ties. That's been the case for the Pawlewicz family—parents Noretta and Bob, their ten children and dozens of grandchildren—who've been holding their annual reunion at Hollis for twenty-four years.

The Pawlewiczes first learned of Hollis's many opportunities when one of the children attended summer camp in the 1970s. By the '90s, many of the children were old enough to work at the camp. Then came marriages and the next generation of Pawlewiczes. When no one's home was big enough to hold a reunion, someone in the family pitched an idea: What about Camp Hollis?

On Labor Day weekend 1996, thirty-one Pawlewicz family members and twenty extended family arrived at the camp for their first reunion. There were boxes of food to sort and cabins for each family to claim. There were activities to plan; some, like Polar Bear Swim and campfires, were borrowed from the summer program. The first year was fun, and the Pawlewiczes learned a lot. Changes were suggested, which Noretta explained:

> *After a couple years, we became more organized and chose to have a Friday Night Dinner followed by a Welcoming Activity hosted by Bob and me. Prior to the weekend, families were given a task to be completed at home and brought to camp. Our first Welcoming Activity was for each family to come up with a Mission Statement that described what it is you want your family to do and be, and the principles you want to govern your family life.*

Once at camp, the families pulled out Arts & Crafts supplies and created posters to illustrate their Mission Statements. Those were hung in the dining hall, and they set the tone for the weekend. Since then, the Welcoming Activity has been part of each Pawlewicz reunion. In 2006, families were asked this question: "What does our Camp Hollis Reunion mean to us?" Families had no problem answering the question:

> *Camp Hollis is known as Camp Pawlewicz in our home and it is synonymous with family and fun. We cherish the extended time we get to spend with the entire family without interruption. It is especially important for the children. You can feel their excitement as the reunion draws near…*
>
> *Camp Hollis is part of our family. It is revisited throughout the year at our dinner table, in school writing pieces and at family functions. The memories created at this beautiful place are priceless.*

One of those memories has been shared by anyone who's ever stayed overnight at the camp. It's been described in many ways and there are thousands of photographs trying to capture the activity's beauty, but I think one member of the Pawlewicz family described it best: "Watching a Camp Hollis sunset is like a multi-colored blanket flying over the lake."

In the early 1990s, as Camp Hollis approached its fiftieth year of operation, Oswego County wanted to properly honor the camp's successful half-century run. A celebration was in order, and in 1997—the camp actually turned fifty in 1996, but the event planning extended into the following year—a party was held. The county needed a host to fundraise and accept donations for the party; it wouldn't have been ethical to pay for the event with county tax dollars. The anniversary planning committee decided to form a not-for-profit support group to partner with the county, naming it the Friends of Camp Hollis. Two of the founding members of the group, Jane Murphy and Vicki Mather, went to work acquiring its nonprofit status, and after several generous contributions, in July 1997, the two-day event brought hundreds of former staff and campers back to Lewis's Bluff.

Among those who attended was Norma (Clark) Parry, from Camp Hollis's first staff in 1946. Attendees enjoyed a campfire, a Candlelight ceremony and lots of mini-reunions from each Hollis era. There were speeches by county and state officials and members of Judge Sullivan's and Dr. Hollis's families. The Friends of Camp Hollis event was a big success, but the group was just getting started.

In the years following the anniversary party, the Friends group funded improvements to the camp. Its first project resulted from comments made by former staff who'd attended the reunion. While strolling through the new main building, counselors from the camp's early years asked, "What happened to our fireplace?" They had a good point, and the decision was made to install a replica of the original. Funds were raised, and by 1999, staff and campers were once again gathering around a rustic-looking fireplace on rainy evenings.

Next, Friends of Camp Hollis Board president Vicki Mather, a newly certified Master Gardener through Cornell Cooperative Extension, offered her skills to improve the grounds around the camp buildings. Vicki and her family lived just down the road from Camp Hollis, and when she agreed to weed a single flower bed near the main building, she had no idea what was in store for her:

> *It was love at first sight. The woods and the lake view were so beautiful. I thought, hmmm this place could use a little flower TLC. However, flowers weren't exactly what I had in mind because this was a children's camp, and I wanted to do things that were just for children.*
>
> *The pizza garden was the first to go in. The site was not well chosen, as it was originally part of a gravel parking lot. With the help of Joan Cybula, fellow Master Gardener, we ended up digging small triangles within the diameter of a circle, mimicking a pizza. The rest of the gravel we left behind, serving as pathways between the plants. In went tomatoes, garlic, basil and oregano, and marigolds planted around the outside to represent the crust. We wanted something children could instantly relate to and to remind children that pizza comes from plants, not just boxes.*

Next was a sensory garden, filled with plants to touch and smell, taste and see. Fuzzy, prickly, stinky and aromatic plants were chosen, as well as salad and herbs. I wanted a garden they could interact with, a garden that said, "Please touch!"

A butterfly garden followed. It was filled with plants butterflies would be attracted to for their nectar or as host plants on which they could lay their eggs and whose tiny caterpillars would then feed.

I found my happy place at Camp Hollis, weeding and watering and planning. Why did I find it all so inspiring and life-giving? Gardens for children connect them with their role as stewards of the earth. A butterfly garden not only helps the butterflies, it helps children to understand that caterpillars are not just insects to be squished, but creatures of potential beauty to be preserved. I always hoped that kids would not only make new friends at camp, but also meet new flowers that they could love and remember.

Creating imaginative gardens at Hollis continued. Staff member Emily Thomas (2006–11) worked her way from counselor to site co-director, and one of her responsibilities overseeing the camp was its counselor-in-training program. Along with workshops on how to be an effective leader, Emily stressed the importance of giving back to the camp by planting a new garden. When the young teens had completed their work, she added a sign with this quote by author Karen Ravn, connecting the practice of good gardening to effective camp counseling:

Only as high as I reach can I grow
Only as far as I seek can I go
Only as deep as I look can I see
Only as big as I dream can I be.

Since it was first established, the Friends group has offered many opportunities for youth to make camp improvements. With the Friends' Cabin Mural Project, launched in 2003, young artists were invited to create murals on an inside wall of camp cabins. Donations were raised specifically for this project so the artists would be paid for their work, adding a valuable job experience to their résumés. A few of those mural artists have established fulfilling careers that reflect their artistic contributions to Camp Hollis. For Eric Hunn, who began drawing when he was a kid, working on a wall-sized mural of a wildlife scene was a step toward his current job as an artist at a Texas-based video game company:

Thanks to the Friends of Camp Hollis, children enjoy themed gardens found throughout the campgrounds. *Courtesy of the Camp Hollis Archives.*

> *The kind of work I do is all about creative problem solving. You're given a loose outline of a scene, for example, and are asked to turn that into a finished, professional product. I recall drawing a bear in the original design of the Camp Hollis mural that was coming out of a cave and yawning. I was told that the bear looked too scary and would need to change. While the painting I do now is largely digital, that first foray into Hollis mural painting was a good indicator of the flexibility you need as a professional artist.*

Maggie Henry, a successful children's book illustrator, was another artist commissioned to create a cabin mural. Maggie was an Oswego High School student when she undertook her first professional project:

> *I didn't even have my driver's license yet, but I was getting paid to paint what I love. My father, Rich Henry (1975), would drive me to "work"*

and he would often tell me stories about when he was a counselor at Camp Hollis. He has since passed, so those memories mean a lot to me.

My parents and the Oswego community have always provided many opportunities. The cabin mural was both an important experience and a chance to give back to the community that has supported my journey. The experience literally expanded my artistic skills and my perception of art-related careers.

Gardens and murals have been colorful contributions to Hollis, but in 2002, the Friends group was called on to assist it beyond beautification projects. It was asked to help save the camp itself.

What was threatening Camp Hollis was something Oswego County and much of the United States had been burdened with in the later part of the twentieth century. Towns and cities were suffering from the loss of employment opportunities for their residents. Factories, the powerhouse of Upstate New York's financial stability for a century or more, were closing. Without steady income, people lost jobs and homes; some moved away in search of work. Oswego County's tax base shrunk, and the programs it supported, including Camp Hollis, had to figure out how to absorb the loss.

Closing the camp would have been an "easy" way for Oswego County to save money. Unlike its mandated social services and highway maintenance, the county had no obligation to operate a children's camp. There was discussion about ending the Hollis program, but ultimately the county decided against it, instead asking the camp to make budget cuts. First to go was its long-standing bus service, which had been offered to parents for free since the camp was founded. Eliminating it helped trim Hollis's budget. But it wasn't enough.

Circumstances worsened economically for Oswego County, and in 2003, the Legislators again were forced to make a decision on the camp's future. They worried that by closing Hollis, other youth organizations would be unable to provide similar recreational opportunities to families. Although no one wanted to turn their back on a program that had always served the needy, continuing to do so for free was no longer feasible. Oswego City-County Youth Bureau and Camp Hollis staff came up with a plan.

To keep the camp in operation, the county would begin charging a fee for a child's attendance. Legislators knew that for some parents who'd recently lost a job or had been struggling before the economic slump, paying for camp would be one more burden. To help ease that financial strain, cost was determined on a sliding scale, with those in greatest need paying a nominal fee. But for some families, even a small cost would be too much. Inspired by Judge Sullivan's founding principal that no child should be denied a camp experience because of money, the Friends of Camp Hollis offered its help.

The Friends began an aggressive fundraising campaign, which would supplement the sliding scale fees collected and offer full fee coverage to families in great need. News of the ambitious goal was met with a positive response from local banks, businesses and granting foundations. Along with these generous organizations—there are too many to mention by name here—there has also been support from individuals. They include former campers and staff who once benefited from Camp Hollis, like Scott Kedenburg (2000–2002), who decided to pay it forward.

While Scott was attending SUNY Oswego, he organized a ballroom formal on campus. College students showed up in tuxes and gowns to dance for Hollis kids, with all proceeds going to the Friends group. Inspired by Scott's efforts, the Friends of Camp Hollis planned a series of community-based fundraisers; there were golf tournaments, membership drives and talent nights. Then, in 2005, the group learned of a fundraiser that seemed perfect for a program that supported children.

Called Kids-N-Trucks, the daylong celebration honors all things on four wheels—the bigger the better. On the morning of the event, a large parking lot becomes the temporary home for dozens of mammoth machines: snowplows, fire trucks, army jeeps, race cars, emergency vehicles and more. Lined up in rows, they wait as curious explorers, holding a parent's hand, visit each vehicle and study them eyeball to headlight, climb behind their steering wheels and beep horns. Now in its sixteenth year, Kids-N-Trucks has become a fun way to spend a summer day in Oswego County.

In its nearly twenty-five years of existence, the Friends of Camp Hollis has raised more than $250,000 to keep the camp open and carry on its founders' dreams of a summer experience for all children. The unique ways in which the Friends group has been supported continues to amaze its board members. In 2019, the Camp Hollis staff started their summer job by holding an auction. During training week, everyone from lifeguards to kitchen staff brought in an item they thought their coworkers might like: free pizza coupons, PlayStation games and so on. One by one, the items were auctioned off, and by the end of the evening, those young adults had raised $709 for the kids they would spend their summer serving.

All contributions to the Friends have been greatly appreciated, but one in particular stands out. A few years ago, at Kids-N-Trucks, Friends board members met a ten-year-old boy who'd enjoyed his recent stay at Camp Hollis. Following the event, a letter arrived in the Friends' mailbox. It was from the boy they'd met. "I'm sending you my allowance money so other kids can have fun at Camp Hollis like I did," he wrote. Tucked into his letter was a five-dollar bill.

WHAT? I'M IN CHARGE
OF CHILDREN!?

When I supervised Camp Hollis in the 1990s and the first decade of the 2000s, I sent out an annual newsletter, updating alumni on the camp's progress. I continued that communication after I'd retired and joined the Friends of Camp Hollis. Along with reports of new building construction and innovative programs, I liked to include my observations on how camp counseling has changed over the years. In 2016, I wrote:

Another summer at Camp Hollis, the 70th since it was founded, has come to an end. The kitchen has been scrubbed one last time, arts & craft supplies are stored in plastic bins, and the cabins are boarded up for the coming winter. As I take an autumn walk around the campgrounds, something that happened this past July came back to mind. One morning, after attending the previous night's campfire, I read in the newspaper that Patricia (McConnell) Pritchard had passed away. Pat was a counselor at Hollis from 1948 to 1952, in the camp's early years.

I had the pleasure of meeting Pat when we were planning the camp's 50th anniversary celebration. She was so helpful, telling stories about those first few summers at Hollis when she and that handful of staff members managed to create a safe and happy camp for children. "We worked at Camp Hollis because we loved kids," Pat said. "It certainly wasn't because of the money; we got about $12.00 a week."

Reading Pat's obituary hit me hard, especially since we lost another former Camp Hollis staff member this year, Dr. David O'Brien. I often think of Dave and Pat together because they served the same four years at Hollis. They also visited camp together in the summer of 2008, when they accepted my invitation to help with that year's staff training. I wanted Pat and Dave to share with the new group of counselors what it was like to work with children in the 1940s and '50s. I was hoping that they would draw parallels between their staff and this one, 60 years later.

That's just what Pat and Dave did. They talked about the great need of those first campers, which sounded a lot like the children Friends of Camp Hollis served in 2008. Ninety percent of today's campers receive some form of assistance through Social Services, charitable organizations or the Friends' scholarship program. The needs of Oswego County children persist, and when it comes to their stay at Camp Hollis, it's the counselors who make all the difference.

I wrote that last sentence with confidence, because I'd seen it, year after year. It's the counselors who make summer fun for children. A camp can brag about new equipment or kid-friendly meals, but nothing will ever replace what happens when counselors take good care of children.

What is it about summer camp that draws in some young adults? With day jobs that pay a decent wage and don't require a live-in commitment, what keeps teenagers signing up for eight weeks of nonstop childcare responsibilities *and* no air conditioning? Judge Sullivan always had the perfect answer, as his son Mike remembered. "Once, Dave O'Brien went to my dad and said that the counselors weren't being paid enough to give up their whole summer. Dad would respond, 'But it's a whole summer with food, lodging and fun!'"

Judge never had much trouble finding willing teens to work for little pay. Among the camp founder's paperwork is a folder of letters addressed to Sullivan, some written with neat penmanship, others typed on college stationery. The letters were short and to the point: "I should like to work at your camp for needy children" or "I met you at my college last month and you encouraged me to write with my interest in working at Camp Hollis." In those early years, it was an invitation from the judge that got you a job at Hollis. Even H.H. Stevens, a school principal throughout his five summers directing Camp Hollis, still typed a formal request for employment each spring, addressing his letter to "Mr. Sullivan."

There are hundreds of stories about young people who couldn't wait to work at camp. In 1983, when Judy McManus was in charge of Camp Hollis, she received two hundred applications for thirty positions. Jeanette Crouch Raby (1978–82), who grew up idolizing counselors when her mom, Jean Crouch, was the cook, couldn't wait for her turn. Even though Jeanette's first job at Hollis meant long hours as a kitchen helper, she never forgot the perks of employment at a summer camp. "Just imagine being able to run to the lake for a swim to cool off or jumping into a baseball game in the middle of an afternoon. Now those are real fringe benefits!"

Living the 24/7 life of a counselor can make it hard to keep the benefits in mind. But if you look for them, they're there, as lifeguard/counselor Patti Mears (1973–75) remembered:

> *The county's Department of Emergency Services had given Camp Hollis some surplus supplies, including three orange fiberglass rafts. While they weren't something campers could use, we lifeguards patrolled around the lake swim area in them, and when we had a little free time, some of us girl counselors would sit on the side of the raft and shave our legs. We felt so lucky; it was like a trip to Disney World.*

A lot of former counselors considered a job in the out-of-doors a real plus. Jessica Moser (2015–16) made a list of her favorite Camp Hollis sights: "Watching a storm roll in over Lake Ontario, with purple lightning; seeing nightly sunsets and stargazing; spotting a bald eagle for the first time in my life; seeing my first shooting star and my wish coming true."

Each autumn, counselors take their summer full of memorable firsts back to hometowns and college dorms, telling friends stories of life at an overnight camp. A few curious friends decide they want to give counseling a try, although they most likely have no idea what they were getting themselves into. Robert Friel (1958) called his first-time camp counselor experience "the beginning of my social conscience being awakened."

A summer or two of that kind of awareness can go a long way. Many counselors take what they learned at camp and carve out careers. Russ Byer (1991–93) led the Hollis nature program almost thirty years ago and is now teaching science at a Rochester school. Recently, Russ reflected on what the camp taught him: "I can see how it really helped me grow up. It was that interesting time of life when you are transitioning from a child to an adult. We learned how to be parents by running the cabins and I learned how to be a teacher from being an activity leader."

Doing a good job as a counselor also means figuring out how to take care of yourself. The demands of a nonstop schedule can be too much for some.

For others, though, it might turn out to be a blessing. John Baumann shared the reality of what life was like during his teen years:

> I was prone to depression and anxiety and there were times I felt very alone with it, that I was the only one struggling with it. I never was able to share that with anyone while I worked at camp, but it kept me so busy that dark clouds were given no time to gather. As long as I was so tired that I fell asleep immediately, the thoughts would not come rushing in. I was around really positive people and doing a lot of really fun things and it gave me another world to be in. We counselors laughed a lot, more than the kids—100 to 200 laughs a day.

Jeff Von Wald is grateful for a job that focused on children. After Jeff worked several summers at Hollis, he left to pursue his career studies. Due to financial constraints, he was forced to withdraw from college. That, along with a series of other setbacks, left Jeff cynical. Then he came back to camp:

> When I inquired about returning to Hollis, I was secretly quite depressed and mostly looking for a place to live and eat for the summer. But my return to the camp staff ended up being profoundly transformative for me. Not only did I find joy again that summer, but my perception of the world changed dramatically. Part of that change came through playing and having fun with the campers, and finding a sense of purpose in helping to create a positive experience for them. Another part of it was the healing effect of the natural world; spending so much time in nature reignited a sense of wonder in me, and a feeling of spiritual depth.

Many have found a spiritual connection at Hollis. Ali Martin calls the camp "sacred grounds." She spent three summers as a counselor and Arts & Crafts director and recalled her growth in those roles:

> When I first came to camp I remember thinking, What am I getting myself into? Each week, we drove into camp and it felt like eternity passed until we left again. The only signs of outside life were airplanes and boats; camp was a secret world all its own. But Jeff Doran (2003–4, 2008–9), our Director, told us we would be amazed at what could happen in one summer there…and he was right! I learned how to change a wet bed at 4 am and how to occupy several hyper campers in a stuffy cabin, in the pool, by the

bonfire, in the woods and at the breakfast, lunch and dinner table. I gained the skill of being flexible in every situation. I learned how physically and emotionally strong I was.

Working summer camp is often a first step into adulthood. After years of observing our parents, neighbors and teachers, we finally get to try out being a grownup. Counselors at a residential camp get thrown into the role of being an adult, and what Aliya Seward (1999, 2001–2) learned about herself was surprising:

I was younger than most of the others who'd applied to work at camp, so I ended up in the kitchen, making and serving food three times a day, five days a week. I thought my kitchen work would be tedious, but that it would be balanced with my counselor work, which would indeed be the most fun job ever. But the first week with children was difficult. Being a counselor was not the barrel of laughs I'd expected. I eventually looked to my kitchen duty as a way to escape dealing with the problems of the counseling job.

By the end of that tough week, something happened to change how Aliya understood her counselor role:

I sat down and watched the sunset with a child who had hurt his ankle during a game. He talked about his summer, his family, his school and the wonderful time he'd had at Camp Hollis. This was his fifth time attending Hollis, which made him four years my senior in camp experience. With the difficult time I was having, it was hard to understand his excitement in coming back for another year. Then I realized that our conversation and my support for him, a child I barely knew, was what kept him coming back.

What Aliya figured out relatively quickly may take other staff multiple summers to understand: being a counselor requires a consistent focus on the needs of children. Kids come to camp ready to express the fullness of their life. Most hit the ground running, gobbling up every activity a counselor can suggest. Some are a bit apprehensive and need a little coaxing. A few struggle even being at camp. They are the homesick kids, and when counselors have made every attempt to turn a child's homesickness around and failed, they have someone they can turn to, someone who deals with all types of sickness: the camp nurse.

A homesick kid's trip to the nurse's office makes sense; after all, they are home*sick*. So, along with the first-day health checkup, attending to bruises and scrapes and dispensing prescribed meds, the nurse will see children who just…don't feel good. Sometimes, it's the nurse herself who magically cures homesickness. It worked for camper Cliff Dumas, who'd developed a crush on the Hollis nurse. "After first meeting her," Cliff admitted, "I would find reasons to go see her."

Nurses learn to separate make-believe illnesses from the real thing, something Sharon Figiera (2005–11) got very good at. After spending several summers with the 4-H camp program, and then working more than twenty years as a school nurse, Sharon became Hollis's nurse, ready with her own homesick camper plan:

> *I found that ice packs and Band-Aids are a great healer, even if not really needed, because, most of all, I was giving out a mom's TLC. When campers came to my office stating, "I don't feel well," I'd do an assessment. Some were sick, but with others I had a feeling it was homesickness. I'd ask questions about what they liked about camp. Many replied that they missed their cat or dog, then added, "I miss my family, too."*
>
> *At this point, I would talk about camp activities they were missing and what was on the schedule for the rest of the day. Often they were ready to join back in by then, so I'd take them to their group. They'd start running when they saw their friends and guess what? They'd forgotten they were sick.*

Camp nurse Dorothy DeHollander (1998–2001) also had remedies for homesickness. A cup of ginger ale could sooth an upset tummy that she was pretty sure was a result of not being at home. A few sips and a quiet chat as the child rested often did the trick. But, as Dorothy recalled, not always:

Early one week, a homesick fellow was brought to me and no amount of ginger ale would work. He wanted to go home and he made it vocally known! I mentioned to him that once a week there was a campfire and counselors brought marshmallows, graham crackers and chocolate bars. I told the camper about the skits and big singalong. I lamented to him that I had no one to go with to the campfire. "I'll go with you!" he offered, completely forgetting that meant staying one more night at camp. With my fingers crossed, I accepted his offer.

The next evening, as prearranged, his counselor brought the youngster into my office. He took me by the hand, led me to the campfire, found a spot for us to sit and promptly busied himself with making me a s'more. I never mentioned that I saw him drop it, intact, onto some campfire ashes. I ate it with a smile on my face and my formerly homesick camper remained with us the rest of the week. Eating a bit of ash was well worth it.

It isn't just campers who have an occasional need for some TLC. When the full-time challenges of taking care of children gets to counselors, they sometimes stop in at the nurse's office. Dorothy had a remedy for them, too, transforming her office into what she called an oasis. "I'd turn off the overhead lights, open windows and use cooling fans on hot days. This usually happened during a time of the day when I planned for quiet work at my desk and I learned to expect an occasional 'May I come in and talk?' from counselors."

Being ready for any kind of illness is part of the camp nurse's job. So is a concern not normally associated with medical care. Ever since children started arriving at Camp Hollis, some show up sorely unprepared for their stay. They might need a toothbrush or a sleeping bag, and at Camp Hollis, those supplies are kept in the nurse's office. Dorothy remembered one visitor who showed up missing something critical to enjoying camp:

A young fellow walked awkwardly into my office on the first day. The counselor told me he thought the boy could use some footgear. I looked down at the end of the legs standing in front of me to see some sort of tape desperately attempting, without much success, to hold the body and sole of his shoes together. We searched for a pair of sneakers that fit and I smiled through tears watching the youngster walk away with strong, confident and very big steps.

A nurse's skills—medical and interpersonal—are critical to Camp Hollis's success. The same goes for other jobs at Hollis, such as maintenance workers, who have the unglamorous responsibility of keeping camp's buildings and grounds clean and safe. For Assemblyman Will Barclay, whose 120th District covers nearly all of Oswego County, his 1987 Hollis maintenance job was "a lot of mowing lawns and unplugging toilets." Not very exciting, but necessary. Maintenance men like Fred Farley (1989–97) and Bill Cahill (1998) took good care of Hollis after retiring from careers in management. They instinctively knew how to maintain the forty-acre facility. And there was Jerry Rounsville (kitchen, 1999–2006; maintenance, 2007–15), who each summer donated time outside of his maintenance workday to construct an attractive improvement to the campgrounds.

Counselors may be attending college to pursue a career in education or recreation, but those skills may not be fully developed when they arrive at camp. Staff do come with unique hobbies and interests, though, and Hollis has always welcomed their talents. The camp has benefited from baton twirlers, trophy-winning wrestlers and Taekwondo enthusiasts. There have been lots of young adults who play guitar, which has inspired campers to pick up the instrument upon their return home. Some counselors are naturally good at leading campfire. And those who show up at Hollis without any specific talent often decide that they will acquire one before next summer.

In the school year after my first summer as a counselor, I decided to teach myself how to play the harmonica. It was a slow process, and my college roommates suffered through my attempts, but I showed up for that second summer able to play a few folk tunes, which I used to lull my campers to sleep after lights out. I'm not alone in Camp Hollis inspiring me to learn and grow. Patrick Howell (2015–17) also was motivated to take on a challenge after his first summer as a counselor.

Patrick was lacking one skill that made him feel a little out of place at a summer camp. He showed a willingness to try just about all the activities, but when it came to swimming—especially in the deep end of the pool—Patrick held back. As a result of a scary incident in deep water when he was four, he sat out during pool games for the entire Hollis season. Over the winter, Patrick thought about what was holding him back and returned for a second summer with a new attitude:

> *I knew that to be in the deep end I'd have to pass a test of swimming the full length of the pool. When the other counselors heard about my goal, they encouraged me. First, I strapped on a lifejacket and slowly dogpaddled my way into deeper water. That gave me the courage to try it without the floatation aid. When I worked my way from the shallow end to the deep end, I felt myself being kept afloat by my own strength and determination.*

Camper Vision

Acknowledging a challenge or a fear is a brave act. When Patrick shared his inability to swim in deep water with fellow counselors and campers, he gave them the gift of honesty and, with it, the idea that it's okay to look at our own shortcomings. That's an important message, especially for children, who often think of adults as fully formed people. In fact, campers are likely to see their counselors as bigger-than-life heroes.

That's a lot of responsibility for a counselor, even if they'd had experience with younger siblings or babysitting. Being a residential camp counselor is about as close to parenting as you can get, and in the last thirty years or so, Hollis has offered a comprehensive pre-camp training, where new staff learn how to manage groups of children, effective discipline, basic first aid—even how to put out a fire, in a workshop presented by the Town of Oswego Fire Department. Although there is some fun mixed in, like the all-staff baseball game Dave Canfield organized during his years supervising the camp, the training is really a crash course in being a good mom or dad, something a teenage counselor needs. Just ask John Baumann, who was sixteen his first summer on the Hollis staff:

> *I was insecure and too quick to raise my voice at first. I soon found that being entertaining was an effective, if exhausting, strategy to keep control, leaping around like Robin Williams. Day One, the clown act engaged them and put them at ease. Days Two and Three, the kids enjoyed that someone was working to entertain them in the absence of TV. By the evening of Day Four, I'd run through my entire repertoire and they were a little less impressed. If camp had gone more than five days, or happened more than once a year, my whole approach wouldn't have worked.*

One way or another, most counselors figure out how to manage children. Their methods may not always be textbook worthy, but each year's staff finds their way. Sometimes, succeeding in the challenge of childcare was due to someone challenging the staff. That was true in Hollis's early years, when the camp was set up like a military base: rise early, cleanup before playtime, three squares a day and lots of competitions. A few of those rivalries pitted the guy staff against the gals. Marsha Wheeler (1971–72) recalled the "war" between Nat's Rats and Spider's Raiders:

> *The Nat's Rats were the female counselors, named for our leader, Natalie Somers. The Spider's Raiders were the guys and our rivalry began for no reason, but was thoroughly enjoyed by both staff and campers. Nat's Rats even had a theme song, sung to the tune of "Happy Days Are Here Again." In part, it went:*
>
> *Nat's Rats are here again*
> *to bring you joy and cheer again*
> *We're all learning how to swim again,*
> *Nat's rats are here again.*
> *Took their razors, took their clothes*
> *and then we squirt them with the hose…*

Marsha can still list the teams' competitions, which were actually pranks: bathing suits up flagpoles, tossing one another into the pool, a box of frogs let loose in the male staff room and more. Day after day, week after week. As usually happens, that kind of one-upmanship will escalate until somebody, usually the camp director, intervenes. That summer, it was Director Herb Hammond who, one morning at 2:00 a.m., called an all-staff meeting and warned that the pranks must end. "Our antics did slow down," Marsha said, "but they never completely stopped."

Of course, children learn by observation, and campers wanted to be part of the rivalries. Camper Rusty Syrell remembered this event during one of his mid-1970s Hollis summers:

> *There were raids where we ran through the opposite gender dorm. All of our guys ran through, but a counselor had to come back and get me. I had stopped to talk to a girl camper. I thought to myself, we're finally here, what's the rush for departure?*

All summers end, and along with them, the rivalries and pranks. But during a certain era of the Camp Hollis story—the 1990s—the competition wouldn't end until the last night of camp. Jim Hooper remembered a particularly good example:

Often, if our cabin was good, we'd take the kids for a sleep out on their last night. We knew that while our cabin was vacated it would be tormented by other cabins, and one year, on the last night of the summer, the cabin led by counselors Pat Sheffield and Dustin Morris [1994–96] got pranked real good. We used rope to tie everything in the cabin to the rafters, and I mean everything: bunk beds, lockers, blankets and sheets, all suspended above.

Those pranks were all for fun, and it made the hard parts of the job a bit more tolerable. Counselors always managed to find ways to relieve tension, and this book wouldn't be complete without a mention of a certain neighbor of the camp that once catered to counselors looking for a little R&R. It was one of Oswego's favorite watering holes, Nunzi's. Before 1982, when the drinking age went from eighteen to nineteen (and then to twenty-one in 1984), alcohol consumption wasn't frowned upon for older teens, so counselors headed through the woods to Nunzi's for their Kill-a-Keg nights. It's been suggested that the very first trail created at the camp wasn't to study nature, but to hightail it to Nunzi's for a cold one before bedtime.

As troubling as it is to think about inebriated counselors returning to their role as guardians of children, something important was taking place during those escapes to Nunzi's. Through the rivalries, pranks and conversations over a beer, counselors were breaking through the awkwardness of strangers trying to function as a team. In little more than two months, Hollis's group of mostly teens has to learn how to work together, and in order to do that, they have to learn about themselves. Several former counselors mentioned this in their recollections of summers spent at the camp. Kristin Meredith

Galley (1990–95) reflected on what it was like for her, an eighteen-year-old searching for something more:

> *The moment I set foot on Camp Hollis ground, I knew, without reservation, that I had found what I was looking for. I finally had a place where I felt like I truly belonged, and it's funny, because most of the people I met there seemed to be in the very same boat; we were a group of "unfitted" people who fit very nicely together! I felt at home for the first time in my life, and even now, that hasn't changed.*
>
> *I've lived miles away from my camp friends for many years, so our contact is limited to the occasional birthday wish or comment on social media. What I know for sure, however, is that those friendships are cemented through our Camp Hollis experience, and the next time we are together, we will laugh, joke, and reconnect as if no time has passed.*

Russ Byer still cherishes the relationships he made at Hollis:

> *We were so close that we spent our nights off together and I'd never experienced that with other peer groups. I'd been spending 24/7 with the Hollis staff and I wanted to be with them during my free time! My last summer, on the last night of camp, I was struck with this feeling that maybe I was never going to see the staff again. I was upset and went down to the fire circle and sat by myself, crying. Another counselor who I'd become close with came over. She didn't say a word; she just sat with me while I grieved. It felt good to have someone there with me.*

All these years later, Russ credits social media with keeping his Hollis connection alive. "I share memories with the staff and we try to find ways to get together. After 20-some years being away, I still think of them as family."

That family feeling makes sense when you're not only working, but living, with a group of people. Bonds grow deep, and when the world of your new family comes face to face with your other life—your birth family, your friends at school—it can be a little uncomfortable. Counselors will tell that you have to work at Camp Hollis to understand the all-encompassing world that it is. "When other people hear our camp stories," Jim Hooper explained, "we say, 'You had to be there.' No one else can understand it, but we can feel it. Those shared experiences are how relationships are made."

But staff are in the "real world" more than the Hollis world. Summer is just a fraction of a year, and when the rest of the year or the rest of the world

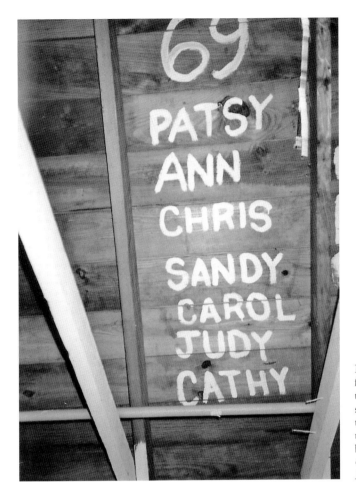

It was tradition for counselors to officially end summer by signing their name in the original main building's rafters.
Courtesy of the Camp Hollis Archives.

doesn't go as planned, counselors keep in mind, as Jeff Von Wald referred of them, "these wonderfully kind and creative people":

> *They were also in the world, which gave me a deep sense of gratefulness for having the chance to be in it with them. All of these reflections came together one evening as we sat around the campfire, the sun setting and the stars emerging, and we sang. That moment is one I'll always remember, particularly when things seem difficult again.*

In my years supervising Hollis staff, I saw many examples of the profound relationships that are created in a single summer. Witnessing this over and over kept alive the memory of my summers as a naïve and insecure counselor. Years later, I turned those feelings into a poem, and although it's about one specific counselor, my lifelong friend Karen Wolbert Allen, I believe it speaks for many:

Camp Friend

On steps still warm from the August sun
we sit outside your cabin,
the night sky—like life—
a breathtaking view,
its many points of wonder
glimmering like the campers entrusted to our care.

It's heaven having a moment to ourselves
after a day so full.
I don't have a clue how to manage kids
and I don't understand all I'm feeling,
but it's pouring out of me now
like meteor showers over the lake,
my troubles tumbling toward unsettled waters

and your open heart
my lifeboat.

When I talk with former counselors, they often say, "It's been fifteen years since I worked at Hollis"—or twenty-five years or forty. It's a way to measure our lives, a way to see ourselves on a moving timeline. But as that timeline lengthens, it can be hard to keep track of when things happened. Fortunately, back in the 1970s, creative staff members came up with a way to memorialize their Camp Hollis years. In the last days of each summer, a few counselors work in secret to create a "staff board": a photo collage of those who worked at Hollis pasted on a piece of plywood, a slice of a tree trunk or weathered driftwood. The board is revealed at the last staff meeting, often to "oohs" and "aahs." Boards often have a theme: the "Raindrops Keep Falling On Our Heads" board offers a clue of the weather in summer 1992, and the "I Will Survive" board in '97 hints at a year with significant challenges.

While preparing for its fiftieth anniversary, attempts were made to assemble staff boards for the camp's earliest years. Efforts were not completely successful, but the camp now proudly displays boards from fifty-five of its seventy-five years. They have become a point of interest for visitors; people spend hours studying them, looking for familiar names or faces.

The boards are also a kind of history lesson for those new to Camp Hollis. When Bill Boyea began working at Hollis in 1984, he studied the boards, and in his five summers at Hollis, he contributed to the tradition. "I was very much into photography and had a camera on me almost 24/7," Bill said. Thanks to staff with an eye for a good snapshot, the fresh faces of each Hollis summer are preserved for all to see.

Counselors have other ways to remember their Camp Hollis summers, including traditional end-of-season staff parties. Everyone who gave their blood, sweat and tears for the children is invited. The party might be a sit-down dinner so staff don't have to serve everyone else before they can eat. Or it might be a road trip to an amusement park, where counselors get to be kids for the day. Some years, the party is right at Hollis, the campgrounds no longer ringing with the sounds of children, the unusual quiet setting the stage for a farewell to summer. I was at one of those parties, back in the '70s, when something so powerful happened I wrote it as a poem:

LEAVING

Children safely on buses heading home,
heavy responsibility finally lifted
from sunburned shoulders,
we gather for the big celebration.
Food galore and—rumor has it—
a watermelon spiked with vodka.

Maybe it's the booze
or maybe the way a last chance feels,
but something gets us going
and the summer starts swirling:
the promise of June
the sweat of July
the missed opportunities of August,
all brewing in this camp cauldron

just as an Ontario storm rolls in
and one of us
—someone called him brave—

stood in the ball field,
weary face to the wind,
feeling it all,
letting reality soak in

till his girlfriend calls him back
right before a slice of lightning
split the old maple by the boys' dorm
clear in half,
proving
without a doubt
that summer was over.

You'll notice my poem includes a girlfriend and boyfriend. It's no surprise that, most summers, two counselors meet and realize that they like each other—a lot. By mid-season, there are usually a half dozen or so summer romances aflame. Most fizzle after the season's final sunset; others turn into lifelong marriages and partnerships. But regardless of how those relationships end, they're another reason working all those hours is worth it. It adds some excitement for counselors, but little do they know that campers are sometimes listening in on those romances, literally. William Dickerson was one of the children paying attention from his cot in the boys' dorm:

The wall at the far end of the dorm didn't go all the way to the ceiling, so counselors on the other side could hear us. I'm not sure if they realized this also meant that we could hear them and some of what we heard was pretty frisky. I suppose they did realize it because when the female counselors sometimes snuck into their room, one would call out in an obviously loud voice, "Girl in the hall." To which others would respond, "Where in the hall is she?" At age ten or eleven, I thought this was wildly funny.

Spending a few weeks as a camp counselor makes a lasting impression on its young staff. After those eventful summers, counselors mature into careers and make new friends; some start a family or devote their personal life to a worthy cause. Although a counselor's Camp Hollis experience rarely intersects with his or her "grown up" life, Tom Roshau found a way to share his life-changing three years at Hollis with his adult coworkers, turning his memories into a Christmas card:

When my turn to move on [from Camp Hollis] *finally came, I took a job working with street kids living in the inner city: kids surrounded by violence, poverty and hopelessness. Although the cityscape seemed light years away from camp, I found time and again that the lessons learned on the shores of Oswego County rang just as true on the streets of Syracuse. I've found that the wisdom of Camp Hollis transcends time and place, whether keeping an eye on the kids in Cabin 11 or keeping an eye on the kids in a broken alleyway. Wherever the twists and turns may lead, I realize now that*

Everything I Need to Know…I Learned at Camp Hollis

- *Everyone matters, even the campers that try to prove otherwise.*
- *Polar Bear Club is a terrific idea at bedtime, but morning arrives way too early. Still, you've got to earn your Polar Bear badge at least once.*
- *Be memorably silly. Cool and camp should never go hand in hand.*
- *No matter how hard you try, forgotten towels will still be hanging on the clothesline after all the campers have gone home for the summer.*
- *When in doubt, go with Blob Tag.*
- *Believe in the campfire stories.*
- *Let the loner-kid find your hiding spot during the Counselor Hunt. He needs the victory more than you do.*
- *Let the same kid strike you out during the final inning of softball. Two victories in the same week are better than one.*
- *Dry socks are a myth.*
- *Learn all the campers by name. They'll remember yours for decades to come.*
- *Laugh as much as possible.*
- *And remember the rules of the camp pool: Walk, don't run. Relax. Take it easy. And never lose track of your pool buddy, keep him close by your side…especially when life finds you in the deep end.*

CAMPERS ARE STORYTELLERS TOO

Whatever conditions prevailed—no money, tough work, 140 hour workweeks—it all seemed to be meaningless because of the kids. They were excited, responsive and lovingly grateful in their own way. Because, for almost all of them, it was their first and only time they'd experienced such things.

Those words, from Judge Sullivan's son Mike, ring true to anyone who's devoted a summer to children at Camp Hollis. There's lots of evidence to support Mike's belief. Tucked away in the Oswego County Records Center is a large box of documents that cover Camp Hollis's early history. Among the newspaper articles, business receipts and activity plans, there is a thick folder containing hundreds of pieces of paper, some with a few sentences scribbled on the back of an old envelope and others formally typed. But they were all addressed to one man, and they all had the same reason for writing: parents were asking Judge Sullivan to select their child for Camp Hollis.

"Please allow my daughter to attend camp this summer," one mother wrote. "Last January, she was sick with rheumatic fever and she lost a lot of weight. Camp would be good for her." Another mother listed the eight children she was raising, and they all wanted their turn at Camp Hollis. Could the judge find it in his heart to select all eight?

In the same folder are paper-clipped pages of school letterhead with the names and ages of children that the school was recommending for camp. In pencil, someone had check-marked several of the names; then, at the

How I Spent
My Summer

"You can always tell which kids went to Camp Hollis."

bottom of the page, that same pencil had added numbers, crossed them out and added again, reconfiguring to include as many children as possible. One of those pages, sent by a school in the spring of 1949, listed thirty-nine boys hoping for a Camp Hollis vacation. Across the top of the page, a note indicated that the camp would only be able to take ten.

Those pencil marks were eventually replaced by computer-driven spreadsheets, but compiling the list of who would go to camp remained a thankless task. During the Health Camp years and the early years of Hollis, the doctor and the judge were made aware of the children most in need; later, the county's Board of Supervisors/Legislators would hear of a child in their district whose circumstances would benefit from a camp session, and those children were among the first invited. But there were always too many hopeful boys and girls and too few spaces. How were the lucky children selected?

Initially, that task would have gone to Judge Sullivan's secretary, Anna May Scott. Those penciled notes and scribbled numbers were most likely made by Anna May, who handled all of the judge's paperwork. "She was a tremendous help getting the children's parents or orphanage staff to fill out applications," Mike Sullivan remembered. "She handled all the formal registration for my dad *and* she collected all the bills to be paid."

For nineteen years, it was the Oswego City-County Youth Bureau's secretary, Janet Murray, who had the job of camper selection. Secretaries are at the center of busy offices, and that was true for Janet, especially in the spring. "Camp Hollis applications were delivered to all Oswego County schools in February and March," Janet explained. "Soon after that, they would start arriving in the Youth Bureau's daily mail—sometimes 100 a day."

Janet would sort the applications by age, gender and dates the child could attend camp. As the weeks went by, the banker box sitting on the floor behind her desk became tightly packed with applications, and by the time it came to select the eight hundred campers who would attend Hollis that summer, the box was heavy with far more than that number. When the day came to make the selection, Janet worked out a process that was fair:

> *I'd take the box home, away from the telephones ringing and regular office business, and use my living room floor to make the selections. I'd spread out*

the sorted applications in several piles facedown, so I couldn't see names, and I'd start randomly picking: week 1, fifty girls and fifty boys; week two, fifty and fifty…

The next day, Janet was back at the office, filling out the eight hundred acceptance letters that would end up in the hands of those lucky children. Keeping the tradition that started with Judge Sullivan, the letter was always addressed to the child. "We wanted to welcome them to Camp Hollis, to make them feel special," Janet said.

Call it the luck of the draw or fate or maybe divine intervention, but eventually the decision of which children are to become campers is made. Statistics from the camp's history show a consistency of where in Oswego County those campers come from: approximately one-third from the city of Oswego, one-third from Fulton and the remainder from throughout the county. Whatever their hometown, those children head off for their temporary summer home carrying a suitcase or backpack and, perhaps, a bad case of the nerves. But they're ready to make memories. And whether those good times were from seventy-five or five years ago, they carry a common theme.

Just getting a place on that Camp Hollis acceptance list could be memorable. Marion Hoffmann, who attended in 1953 and '54, remembered how she was invited. "A lady came to our house and asked my mother if we kids wanted to go to camp. They were canvassing the area for families with impoverished children and ours was one of them. I'd never been off the farm, so to speak, and though my brother and sister declined the offer because they were afraid to leave home, I excitedly opted to go."

Marion's memories endured into her adulthood, influencing her decisions as a mother of three. When her children reached camper age, Marion asked that they be given a chance to attend Camp Hollis. "We were poor at the time," she said, "and the camp took low-income kids. Now, my children also have memories they will never forget."

For decades, once the invitation to attend camp was extended and accepted, there was the bus trip that took kids to Hollis. For Pat Cloonan, who attended the camp in the late 1950s, "the bus ride there was exciting. I'd never ridden on a school bus before because I went to the Catholic school in my neighborhood." Two weeks later, the bus ride back found Pat a changed boy. "When I got home I remember thinking how small my house looked after living at the camp. It had been my first time away and I had to readjust to being back home."

Children get one more look at Camp Hollis as their bus leaves to take them home. *Courtesy of the Camp Hollis Archives.*

Linda Jessmore's five years at camp, from 1956 through '60, began with a ride on that bus, and she had no idea where it was taking her. "Getting there was all wilderness," she remembered. "It wasn't until my husband brought me out to see Camp Hollis that I was able to figure out where it was."

Linda has two more memories of the Camp Hollis bus. She and the other campers rode one to a Catholic church in Oswego, where she attended her first wedding. "One of our counselors, Betty Henderson [1960], was married during the summer and all the campers were there, wearing our camp T-shirts." Then there was the final bus ride, at the end of Linda's session. As campers boarded the bus, many were in tears. "They shouted from windows, promising to write their favorite counselor."

Some would keep that promise. By the last weeks of summer, a counselor would be sent to Hollis's mailbox, where an armful of letters would be waiting. Most were written by parents of children attending camp, but a few had a counselor's first name printed above the camp address. Here's one found in camp history paperwork: "Mike," the camper wrote, "I love the ghost stories you told. I'm coming back to Camp Hollis next year and I want to be in your cabin."

On that bus ride home, Linda found a way to keep her Hollis memories alive. "I was from Fulton and had never met children from Oswego. At camp, I made friends with some of them and we became pen pals."

173

"There goes the last bus of the summer.
....Now what do we do?"

Meeting on a bus to Camp Hollis could sometimes result in more than a letter-writing friendship. In Hollis's first year, ten-year-old Barbara Main was chosen from the Oswego Children's Home to attend the new camp. While on the bus, she saw nine-year-old John Chesare, from a poor family in Oswego. "We made eye contact," John remembered. "I think her eyes really got me." The two spent as much time together as they could during their stay and then reunited at Camp Hollis for the next few summers. "We swam together, played sports together and had our first kiss on the camp trails," Barbara said. That kiss "sealed the deal" for John and Barbara, who were married in 1955 and showed up for camp's fiftieth anniversary holding hands, looking forward to walking the trails again.

Counselors meet hundreds of children each summer, which can make remembering who's who a bit of a chore. But it was a challenge Doug Roshau was ready to tackle. Doug made a pledge to learn the names of all campers by their first afternoon at Hollis. Some children had names that were easy for counselors to remember. Sarah Gould Hill still thinks of one of her campers, Sarah Darling, as "Sarah 2," while she was known as "Sarah 1."

Memories of children from the orphanages are among the most poignant reminders of what Camp Hollis can do for a youngster. Their stories can be as humble as Clinton Hulett's, who looked forward to leaving the Oswego Children's Home, where they "only had a rundown jungle gym, just slides and swings. Camp Hollis was all playground." And for orphans who had to share any adult attention with dozens of other children, Camp Hollis offered comfort along with the fun. "Sometimes, a child would cry or wake up scared in the middle of the night," Christine Fisher remembered. "A counselor would come and I could hear her whispering quietly to the girl while rubbing her back to soothe her pain and fears."

William Dickerson credits Camp Hollis as one of the reasons he was able to move beyond the orphanage's way of life and achieve success in his adulthood:

One thing that saved me during my forlorn childhood was my ability to recognize the presence of hopeful beacons along the way: people who would treat me with kindness and respect. I used them to grow toward the light of my own positive future possibilities. Camp Hollis was one such beacon.

There were other ways that Hollis helped children who'd been raised in institutions. Here's an anonymous comment sent to an online newspaper that had run an article about the camp. The parent wrote:

Our only child, adopted from eastern Europe, had a unique experience her three summers at the camp. The first time, she reconnected with the part of herself who had lived, slept and ate with other children. She enjoyed much about her American life, but this part of her early life she craved and missed a great deal. Unable to afford another foreign adoption, this was not something we could give her. So Camp Hollis gave her "siblings" for a week!

Children have a way of finding something or someone at Camp Hollis to make their experience special. Terri Burns, a camper from 1959 until '61, fondly remembered a counselor named Pat, "but," she explained, "we used to call her Ma." Being cared for sometimes looks like a hearty breakfast, lunch or dinner, so there have been plenty of campers who think of Hollis as overflowing with love. "I grew up having feelings of despair when we were hungry or when our house was cold," Ted Baker said. "I'd go to school feeling deprived by our circumstances. But Camp Hollis had all this food and we could have as much as we wanted. Going to camp made me feel very special."

Rusty Syrell also knows what it was like to feel special at Camp Hollis. Rusty grew up in Oswego, and as he remembered it, "I played and lived hockey in the winter, so for me summer was just my own personal waiting room until I could be skating again." But Rusty's older brother, Bill, kept telling him how great Camp Hollis was. Finally, Rusty got his chance to find out for himself. "I was as anxious for my week at camp as I was for the first Zamboni pass of the hockey season."

Rusty made lots of Hollis memories: "During campfire singalongs and stories we would be transported to unknown lands, where quicksand really was near us, so we had to make sure to stay on the trails." There was the Hollis Hop, where "all of the week's shy flirting allowed for more awkward, act-or-it-may-be-too-late feelings." During a water balloon toss, Rusty came out the victor. Later that night, during a movie, "the kitchen staff brought me my very own ice cream sundae." But best of all, Rusty said, were the grownups he met at camp:

> *There were counselors at Hollis who invoked in me a feeling that I was very very special and for no other reason than because I exist. Sometimes in life we meet someone or go to a place or experience something that has life-changing impact in a most positive way. Those three things came together for me at Camp Hollis. When it was time to go home, we'd exchange contacts (home phone and address back then) and we'd look forward to summer next year. For me, it meant that more than hockey existed in my life.*

Reports of what Hollis was providing children reached adults back home who were responsible for the camp's success. Oswego County Legislators, looking to make sure local tax dollars were being put to good use, talked with parents and toured the campgrounds to observe for themselves. Legislator Hollis Iselin, who was a frequent visitor during his years representing the town of Schroeppel, shared this memory of the camp when it celebrated its fiftieth anniversary. It's the story of a young girl from Iselin's district who'd enjoyed her Camp Hollis stay so much that she couldn't forget about it, long after she'd returned home:

> *This girl kept calling me, begging for me to take her back to Camp Hollis, even though it was closed for the season. I finally caved in, and when we arrived at the camp, the girl jumped out of my car and ran to the lake. I found her clutching a rock to her chest. She'd painted it while she was a camper that summer. This girl was homesick for camp.*

Returning to Camp Hollis is a goal for many children. A few from Oswego hop on bicycles and pedal through city streets and country roads to spend a few hours back at camp. Even luckier were children from the Camp Hollis neighborhood, like young Jack "Rocky" Knutson, who lived at the end of Health Camp Road. Rocky had the unique experience of waking up every day during the summer, ready to have fun with a hundred playmates.

There are children so taken by the Camp Hollis experience that they vow to become counselors when they're old enough. That's how it worked for Danielle Barriger Lewis, who, as a camper from 1994 through '97, found that "everything was exciting: the arrival, cabin assignments, activities, campfires." Danielle also loved how, on the last day of camp, counselors preserved those memories by signing campers' Hollis T-shirts. "They would always write a fun thing from the week." Also keeping her memories bright was a strong connection Danielle made with a counselor named Heidi. "We ended up being pen pals for a couple years."

Even after young Danielle moved to Florida in 2000, camp remained a happy memory. As she neared her high school graduation, she settled on her career goals. "I knew from my experience at camp and an awesome teacher in elementary school that I wanted to major in education." Upon earning her degree from the University of South Florida, Danielle was ready for a vacation. She had an idea. "I knew I'd be spending my summer in New York, but I also needed to work. What better job to have than something I'd wanted to do since I was a kid: be a counselor at the best camp ever!"

Danielle contacted Camp Hollis, filled out a work application and landed a phone interview. She enthusiastically shared her memories of being a Hollis camper, now wanting to give something back as a young adult. Danielle got her dream job and described what happened as soon as she pulled her car into the camp parking lot:

> *Though I was a couple years older than the other counselors, I was instantly welcomed, which is how I always remembered Camp Hollis. It's a place of acceptance. I learned a lot in my first summer back: how to make a grass whistle, how to plunge a toilet, how to handle an entire cabin of girls going through girly stuff, how it didn't matter what kind of skit or song you did at campfire, how it's okay to depend on others to help you along the way and how, no matter the situation, my opinion matters.*

Danielle met her husband while in New York State, and after completing a second year of camp, she became pregnant with their first child. Her time as a counselor had come to an end, so you might imagine that would also be the end of her Camp Hollis story. But it's not.

Eight years later, Danielle sent her daughter, Janelle, to the Camp Hollis overnight. She worried about her firstborn. "Janelle's kind of a wildcard when it comes to her likes and dislikes. She's a very picky eater, so, as much as I wanted her to love camp, I knew there was a chance she wouldn't."

Like many worried moms, Danielle's fears were unfounded. Janelle so enjoyed the overnight that she signed up for Hollis's weeklong program the next summer. That year, Danielle's youngest, Jaydance, became a Camp Hollis lover just like her mother and sister. Soon the whole family was singing camp songs and performing skits, using stuffed animals and family pets to round out the cast. And in the spirit of "like mother, like daughter," Janelle is already counting the days until her fifteenth birthday, when she'll be old enough to spend her summer as a Hollis counselor-in-training.

"Here's how I sum up my three Camp Hollis experiences, first as a camper, then as a counselor and now a parent," Danielle explained. "Though each experience can be described differently, there's just one feeling. No matter the age or time period you experience Camp Hollis, it is and will always be an amazing adventure!"

Often, the importance of attending Camp Hollis can only be expressed years later, from an adult's perspective. But now and then, children find the right words. In 2009, staff member Ali Martin asked her cabin how they'd remember their week at camp. Here's one eleven-year-old's answer: "Camp Hollis has taught us how to be ourselves, find our inner beauty, find trust in others and to never let go of our dreams. Camp Hollis will always be a part of us."

Thirteen-year-old Emily Stacey decided to write a letter to the entire 2016 staff after her week at camp: "You go to camp expecting to make friends, but you end up with family. That's the magic of Camp Hollis. The people, the laughs, the fun and the connections. It gets hold of your heart and never lets go."

Young Emily is right, because, for adults like Rima Stitch, memories of Camp Hollis continue to help, long after she'd been a camper:

> *I was a troubled child, so my therapist thought going to camp would be a great way for me to make friends. Now when I look back on my summers as a kid, it's Camp Hollis that I think of. I would get so excited when my mom would get the paperwork for camp. My brother and I were a year apart, so it was fun to go together. We would come home and talk my parents' ears off for days and then count down the months till we could go back. My little sister started attending camp last year and I got so excited to sing the songs with her and hear about her week. Hiking the trails was my favorite part; they were always so beautiful. To this day, when I've had a bad day I go out and hike.*

Making sure that children have memories to last a lifetime is the responsibility of Oswego County Legislators, who, year after year, continue to support and provide funding for the camp. It's the job of Oswego City-County Youth Bureau employees, who research and develop new programs that keep kids coming back. It's the job of summer staff—counselors, kitchen

workers, nurse—who welcome each camper into the Hollis family. And it's the job of the Friends of Camp Hollis, who make sure that no child is ever turned away because of financial constraints.

Among those who've served as a Friends of Camp Hollis board member is Debbie Ellingwood Buske. Debbie joined the board because of her many memories as a Hollis camper. She remembered winning archery awards, sleeping out in lean-tos, listening to ghost stories about the old bus in the woods and going 'round and 'round on the camp's maypole. "Those two weeks at Camp Hollis were the best part of my childhood," Debbie explained. "I was the oldest child in my family and had a lot of responsibility at home. When I arrived at Camp Hollis, all that responsibility melted away. I could have fun."

It all comes down to that one word, doesn't it? Fun. Give children a vacation from challenging family situations or tough social circumstances and you'll have offered them an opportunity to see life—and themselves—in a better light. Like Debbie, there are thousands of us who found respite at the camp on Lewis's Bluff. The little haven on the water, it turns out, has given kids enough happy memories to fill a Great Lake.

Epilogue

THE ROAD AHEAD

One might wonder, as Camp Hollis celebrates its seventy-fifth anniversary and the Health Camp's founding approaches its century mark, what lies ahead for the camp on Lewis's Bluff? Does a world that relies on technology to keep spinning still have a purpose for outdoor recreation programs? Now that most communities provide a variety of youth activities, why send a child away from home? And with concerns of an international pandemic threatening our health and safety, should youngsters even be gathering in groups? Sure, there are plenty of opinions suggesting that going to summer camp has outlived its usefulness, but there's one important reason why it has not.

I became convinced of that reason toward the end of my career at Camp Hollis. Boys and girls were showing up at camp wondering where the computers were. A few parents were insisting that their children needed to carry a cellphone 24/7. One camper, when told we wouldn't be playing video games at camp, asked, with fear in his eyes, "But what am I gonna do?" Without electronics, this boy did not know how to play.

Research supports my theory that many of today's children have lost their ability to play freely. In the book *Last Child in the Woods*, author Richard Louv documented the alarming truth of how children now spend their leisure time. It isn't the amount of time kids are using devices that's revelatory—it's Louv's research of how it affects a child's physical and emotional development. Electronic-savvy kids have shorter attention spans. They have trouble understanding and controlling their emotions. They can't seem to relax. What most of us learned back in "the good old days" has now been confirmed by science: to mature into healthy adults, kids need time outdoors.

Along with observing how too much technology harms young people, I also witnessed how "easy" it is to reverse that negative impact. After a few days or weeks spending sunup to sundown playing in nature, I saw a change in children. There were more smiles. There was a healthy glow to young faces. Some days it seemed like the whole camp was exhaling. Although Dr. Hollis and Judge Sullivan would surely be shocked to learn that an overdependence on electronics is the main threat to the health of today's children, they would surely agree that nature is where we can heal from it.

Getting kids outside as much as possible reminds me of an idea to improve Camp Hollis that I first had forty years ago. Although it was designed to be of benefit to kids, I have to admit that there was a selfish reason behind my idea. In the fall of 1979, I'd graduated college and completed my sixth season on the Hollis staff. Like many who loved their sleepaway summers, my days of surviving on a part-time job needed to end. It was time to say goodbye to camp, but I wasn't ready to let go. I had a plan.

After years of observing the array of experiences that Camp Hollis could provide, I began thinking about what could happen if we expanded those opportunities beyond the borders of summer. I pitched my idea to Youth Bureau director Steve McDonough: If he would allow me to stay at the camp into the autumn season, I would research the feasibility of operating Hollis as a year-round facility. Steve gave me the green light, and I began meeting with school administrators, human services personnel and youth leaders, hoping to drum up interest in a camp for all seasons.

The discussions were promising, and as the daylight hours dwindled and October winds blew in over the lake, I sat by the indoor fireplace and dreamed. I added layers of clothing and kept my head down as I walked the grounds, visualizing the fun children could have in winter. It wasn't until that first frosty morning left a layer of snow on playground equipment that I got a dose of reality. As much as I loved the camp on Lewis's Bluff, it couldn't keep me warm through an Oswego winter. I packed my duffel bag, rented an apartment in town and, six months later, landed a teaching job out of state. I said goodbye, I thought, to Camp Hollis.

In 1989, after realizing that classroom teaching wasn't the best fit for me, I was overjoyed to learn Oswego County had created a full-time position in its Youth Bureau department that included oversight of Camp Hollis. I applied for the job and began a new association with the camp, one that gave me another twenty-one summers at Hollis. Those were busy years, and every once in a while the idea of turning the camp into a year-round facility resurfaced. But my life was in a different place. I'd married and was a dad to two children, and my energy level, once as boundless as a Great Lake, no longer was excited about twelve-hour days twelve months a year. But some dreams just won't die.

In 2013, Brian Chetney was appointed Youth Bureau director, assuming the role of addressing the shifting needs of Oswego County kids. Brian and his wife, Julie, have sent their four children to Camp Hollis, so he's quite familiar with the stories about its traditions, staff, games and songs around the campfire. Knowing the importance of outdoor fun for children, Brian has been overseeing improvements to the campgrounds. Along with work on Hollis's forty-year-old pool, renovations in the dining hall and upgrades on the cabins, Brian is currently involved with two impactful upgrades for the camp, both announced in 2019.

First is a New York State grant awarded to Oswego County that will provide funding to address the camp's long history of bluff erosion. As part of the state's Lake Ontario Resiliency and Economic Development Initiative, the camp will receive $500,000 to stabilize its shoreline and stop the erosion that has swept away acres of the county property. Work on this project is slated to begin in 2021.

The second initiative that would move Hollis into a new era came shortly after Chetney hired Zach Grulich as the latest coordinator of Parks & Recreation for Oswego County. Though new to the position, Zach was quite familiar with Camp Hollis. His mom attended the camp as a child and made sure that her children gave it a try. Zach needed only one visit to convince him that Camp Hollis was where he wanted to be:

> *I went to the 8-year-old overnight in 1997 and had a great time. I remember my counselor Tessie was an interesting character. He wore funny hats and was quick on the sports field. After I watched him fool everybody during Capture the Flag, I decided I wanted to be a counselor someday.*

Zach was a camper every year he was eligible and then began volunteering at Hollis, including doing time in the kitchen. Whenever he had a free moment, he'd stand in the dining hall and look at the staff boards, dreaming of the day when his picture could be on one. That chance came when he was seventeen. "I'd gotten my lifeguarding certification and was hired for a summer at Hollis, starting the day after I graduated from high school."

Hollis directors saw Zach's abilities in youth and recreation programming, and he got promoted each summer, becoming the sports activity leader and then, at age twenty, co-director of the seasonal camp. Three years later, with a college degree in physical education, Zach moved on from Camp Hollis. He ended up working at several YMCAs in the northeastern United States. They had day camps, but for Zach, they were nothing like Hollis. It became his dream that someday he might return to the camp on Lewis's Bluff. In 2019, Zach got his wish.

"After I interviewed for the job," Zach explained, "I had my resignation letter typed up and ready to go—just in case." It was a smart move. On January 21, Zach worked his last day at the YMCA; he was at his Youth Bureau desk on January 22. While overseeing the 2019 camp season, Zach began formulating his personal goals for Hollis.

"I want to bring back some traditions that have been part of the camp since its beginning," he said. "Activities like the Kohanna stick and tent sleep outs in the woods." He acknowledged the camp's need to engage with technology, working with social media to spread the word about camp fun. He stressed his intent to hire the best staff, "like my counselor Tessie, who was willing to go above and beyond the standards and be a life-changing role model for kids." Then Zach offered one final goal, one I was overjoyed to hear. "The best way to accomplish these goals," he stressed, "is to make camp a year-round destination, where kids can enjoy the facility in every season."

Zach and I talked about the possibilities of a year-round camp, and it felt like a former camp director was just trading dreams with the current director. By the end of November, though, Zach had contacted me with some exciting news. The County of Oswego had received a second substantial grant, this one through New York State's Consolidated Funding Application. The $229,000 grant from the New York State Parks, Recreation and Historic Preservation will support the winterization of Hollis's main building, allowing the camp on Lewis's Bluff to welcome visitors every month of the year for the first time in its history.

After hearing the exciting news, I drove out to camp. It was late fall, and the buildings were boarded up. As I walked the grounds, I wondered if this might be the last time camp would sit sleepy and silent. I imagined children sledding on the hill near the main building and creating snowmen to stand guard outside each cabin. I thought of hot cocoa parties by the indoor fireplace. Things sure were looking up for Camp Hollis, I thought. But the world, it turned out, had something else in mind.

In early March 2020, while Zach was preparing for the seventy-fourth summer at Camp Hollis, he learned the disturbing news of a new virus compromising the health of an alarming number of people. A few weeks later, life as we knew it shut down. Communities were in crisis, and among the many questions parents were asking about their children's future was this: Would there be a Camp Hollis in 2020?

There were many considerations Zach, the Oswego County Health Department and County Legislators had to figure out in those spring months, as the calendar crept closer to summer. While health experts were still learning how COVID-19 affected those who contracted the virus, Zach was trying to imagine a new Camp Hollis, one where children could still have fun and grow healthy while he and his staff made sure everyone followed safety measures. Was doing so even possible?

As this intense learning curve continued, I was finishing the final edits of this book, and as I read and reread the origin story of the camp on Lewis's Bluff, I recognized the strong connection between what was happening in 2020 to Dr. Hollis's Health Camp. The doctor was a leader in the battle against tuberculosis, a disease that attacks respiratory systems and is transmitted from person to person, which makes TB seem an awful lot like the grandfather of COVID-19. Almost one hundred years after health camps saved lives, medical professionals were again trying to protect children from a deadly disease. Was there a way that Camp Hollis could help?

It wasn't until May that Oswego County came up with a plan for Hollis to operate in the coming summer. While providing an overnight camp for children was too risky—those cabins are great for making friends but tough for maintaining social distance—having a day camp with a reduced number of children would be allowed. Zach got to work training his staff with some new protocol.

Summer 2020 was surely different for Camp Hollis. Every day started with a temperature check of all campers and staff. The already-frequent handwashing was supplemented with hand sanitizer stations. Family-style meals were replaced by children sitting six feet apart. But a few things remained the same. Here's how Alexis Richer (2018–20), who served as the camp's site director during Hollis's new day camp, explained what providing fun during a pandemic meant:

> *While this summer wasn't what we had expected and wanted, we were able to give our campers and counselors a Camp Hollis experience that will surely be unforgettable. The guidelines restricted us in many ways, but*

185

empowered us to be incredible in so many others. The masks may have hid our smiles, but our energy excited the campers. This summer wasn't what we had expected, but it's what we needed. As one parent said, our staff had created a program that was titled for so many as "Camp Covid Rehab."

Since retiring from Camp Hollis, I've shifted to taking care of its gardens, which allows me to visit the camp regularly. I continued doing so in the summer of 2020, and it sure sounded good to open my car door and hear children laughing and engaged in activities. One day after gardening, I got back in my car, and like I always do, I adjusted the rearview mirror to take one last look at the campgrounds, storing it like a photograph for those days when life gets to be too much. I pulled out of the parking lot, moving slowly—not just because I was on the lookout for critters, but because something was pulling at me. It always feels that way, like someone started a boondoggle back at the first camp on Lewis's Bluff and all of us who helped weave it are still holding on.

BIBLIOGRAPHY

Articles and Books

Annual Sessions of the Oswego County Board of Supervisors/County Legislators. Oswego County, Oswego, New York, various years.

Fisher, Frank. *Unloved, Oswego Children's Home.* Chicago: Publisher Services, 2016.

Hollis, Dr. LeRoy F. "Our Golden Wedding Day, 1893–1943." Program, Sandy Creek, NY, 1943.

Louv, Richard. *Last Child in the Woods: Saving Our Children from Nature-Deficit Disorder.* New York: Algonquin Books of Chapel Hill, 2005.

Martin, Betty D. *Orwell Remembered.* Pulaski, NY, 1976.

Otis, Paul C. "Founding of Children's Camp Traced to Chance." *Post-Standard*, August 23, 1953.

Spellman, Jane Ann Sullivan. *Fifty Years of Camp Hollis Memories, 1946–1996.* Oswego, NY: Oswego County Youth Bureau, 1997.

Newspapers

Fulton Patriot
Mexico Independent
Palladium Times

Pulaski Democrat
Sandy Creek News
Valley News

Website Resources

Maynard, Mickey. "Alewives, a Dark Cloud of Bait with a Silver Lining" http://www.angelfire.com/home/lake/alewife2010.html.

New York State Historical Newspapers. https://nyshistoricnewspapers.org.

Old Fulton New York Postcards. fultonhistory.com.

Oswego County Comprehensive Plan. http://oswegocounty.com/pdf/ compplan.PDF.

Silveira, John, and Richard Blunt. "Chimney Bluffs—Glacial Art on Lake Ontario." Where We Live series, *Backwoods Home Magazine* blog, August 4, 2014. www.backwoodshome.com/blogs/WhereWeLive/2014/08/04/ chimney-bluffs-glacial-art-on-lake-ontario.

USDA Natural Resources Conservation District. "Custom Soil Resource Report for Oswego County, Camp Hollis." June 28, 2019. https:// websoilsurvey.sc.egov.usda.gov/WssProduct/qfzcjzacdlnu0ztxjz2sdyt1/ GN_00001/20190628_10045910768_26_Soil_Report.pdf.

ABOUT THE AUTHOR

Jim Farfaglia lives in and writes about the history and traditions of Upstate New York. In 2011, after a fulfilling career directing a children's camp and advocating for youth, Farfaglia transitioned to focusing on his lifelong interest in writing. Splitting his time between poetry and what he calls "story-driven nonfiction," Jim also enjoys helping others fulfill their dream of writing a book. Visit his website at www.jimfarfaglia.com.